By Nincy Erazo
Edited by Liz Sarmiento

Resilience
The Nincy Erazo Story

By Nincy Erazo

Edited by Liz Sarmiento

ISBN-10:   1-6700-7631-8
ISBN-13:   978-1-6700-7631-1

Printed in United States of America.

Dedication

I dedicate this book to my children. They are my inspiration and reason for writing. I thank my sister and parents for their invaluable help with research and for being so supportive in this dream come true. I pray that this is the beginning of more books to come, with God's guidance and the support of my wonderful family.

Nincy Erazo

Table of Contents

Introduction

Resilience shows the journey of life through the lens of a young girl becoming a woman, beginning with her earliest memories and most treasured moments, and continuing to her daily thoughts and experiences. It is to be read as a dairy, with entries of everyday life. The reader will witness growth and maturity in both a physical and emotional sense. The hope is that these simple writings will inspire someone who may be suffering one of the many struggles that the author has endured. A key focus is to show how one might end up in an abusive relationship, and what that entails. There is no direct path by which you enter such a relationship. I wrote this with the intent of reaching out and hopefully helping someone. You will see the vicious cycles of abuse and what it takes to break free from it. Part of the story is about over-coming child molestation and the process it takes to not be defined by it. The story involves abandonment issues, adultery, infidelities, and brokenness that can destroy. Yet we can all be more than conquerors. God has given us all a spirit of Resilience.

"For God gave us a spirit not of fear but of power and love and self-control. Therefore do not be ashamed of the testimony..." (II Timothy 1:7–8a ESV).

Chapter 1

Origin

I was recently asked to describe myself using just one word, and the word that came to my mind immediately was *resilience*. Psychological resilience is the ability to emotionally cope with a crisis or to return to pre-crisis status quickly. Resilience exists when the person uses "mental processes and behaviors in promoting personal assets and protecting self from the potential negative effects of stressors" (Wikipedia).

During my life I have been abused, hurt, taken advantage of, and simply damaged. I have suffered much pain, both physically and emotionally. I have lived in guilt, shame, and embarrassment because of things I endured. Through certain things that have happened to me I have thought of myself as disgraceful.

Many things arose from my own fault and bad decision making, while others have been things that were out of my control, that were predetermined. I have learned to see things in certain ways. I can acknowledge the events that challenged me and made me grow. I treasure all of my struggles and paths.

I am grateful for everything that I have ever gone through. I like to think of them as adventures. Adventures and experiences in which I was given all the correct answers and paths to choose from, however I diverted. I am a strong believer in faith and destiny. I sometimes feel that I have already lived my life and I am now somewhere up in heaven watching over myself. I try to envision life from another angle, one in which I have all the wisdom in the world and now have another chance at life. I think of my conscience as my older self that is trying to make me see what is important and come to a better conclusion.

I want all the same things I have in my life now but some things I would have preferred to not live through. I know that it does not work that way. We cannot have triumph in our lives without the despair. Life is composed of good and bad. There is a famous saying I really like:

"Stars can't shine without darkness."

I know that the bad is necessary in our lives. It is essential for us for us to grow. When I reflect on my life I am filled with joy and sorrow and the same time. The events that broke me were the same ones that made me stand up and fight. I have always considered myself a weak person. I have always thought that I will not make it out of the tough situations. I have never believed in myself because I think I am not enough. Due to the outcome of my own decisions I tend to doubt my own judgment. I can see at the exact moment things went bad for me.

Upon reflection of my memories, I start to differ from my thoughts. I want to share some of my greatest memories in this book. The most dramatic and earliest memory I have is the following:

Today is Saturday, October 19, 1985. However, it does not feel like fall. It is merely another hot and sunny day. It is very hot. There are no leaves on the ground, nor trees that are bare. Tall palm trees and swamps are all that surround us. I have never known any other type of weather, living here in the south. Only on television have I seen white fluffy snow over mountain tops and trees. I have never seen the real thing. I have never felt the cold breeze or frozen fingertips, like how they describe on the radio.

I dream of one day touching the snow. I dream of seeing the frozen rivers and lakes. I also want to step on grass that is covered in snow. I hope one day to feel the cold air and have the need to wear warm clothes. I want to see my warm breath in the air when I speak. I have never experienced these things because where I live, it does not get cold. I live in the southern part of the United States, in Shreveport, Louisiana, where the sun is so hot that all of your body feels sticky, and you feel like your skin is burning. Every day is like this, and I am fine with it. I take a shower and when I step outside my hair is immediately dry, which is hard to do since I have a thick head of tight, black curls. Usually not even a towel can dry it that fast. However, the sun does the job of a blow dryer.

My mother says this is the same type of weather she grew up in. My mother was born in Guatemala in the early sixties. I was born in Guatemala also, but our mother brought my sister and me to the United States when I was only three years old. I do not remember much about that; my mother says we left in the pursuit of having a better life here. She says that she brought us along with her youngest brother to make sure we had better lives. Our lives are great here because we have everything we could ever need. We have nice clothes, toys, food of our choice, a big two-story house with our very own beds. We have it all.

My mother is very brave. She is my superhero. For as long as I can remember she has been a solid foundation for me during my early years. She has always given me an example to follow, not by words but by actions. She speaks of awful times when the *guerrilleros* (guerrilla soldiers) would come into people's homes and kill or take who they could to fight in the war. I am blessed that I do not remember such times. My mother tells us how fortunate we are to live in the United States and how safe we are here. I feel badly for those that do not have what we have. Our mom worked very hard before she brought us here, but it was not enough because she could not provide enough for food and shelter. She found herself forced to bring us across all of Mexico then into the U.S. She also brought her youngest brother, James. He was only fourteen years old at the time.

Coyote is a slang term for someone who smuggles people across international borders, particularly through Mexico to the U.S. My mother did for us the job of a coyote. She took it upon herself to figure out the best way to cross the border without getting stopped and caught. She crossed us illegally into the United States. She tells us how difficult it was, but ultimately she survived, so we did as well. I have always heard of horror stories of crossing the desert to get here. Friends of my parents that tell stories of how they found dead bodies, or of people who lost body parts. Some families get separated during raids. I cannot imagine what it would be like to be somewhere hiding and watch everyone run in different directions and getting separated from my sister and mother. We have heard of people suffering immensely and even dying. My uncle, James, was told that he had to ride in the trunk of a car for an extensive amount of time. My mother said no and did not let them put him in. She knew that he would die in there along with the others that were placed there as well. The man in charge of the group got upset and left us there. He did not care that my mom had paid him already, and he was supposed to take us farther. He said if we did not do what he said then he was not going to bother with us either. Thankfully, my mom found another way to get to the next safe place. It took her two weeks to get us all from Guatemala to Louisiana. I do not know where she got the courage and bravery to keep going with us, but she did.

My sister and I were tired and hungry from the long trip from Guatemala to the U.S., but she somehow found the way to keep us cheerful and strong enough to keep going. As a child we do not see our parent's sacrifices and struggles. All we ever manage to see is the bed and house we live in, the food that we eat, and the clothes that we are dressed in. Our parents did the best they could with us.

My mother is a beautiful, tall, elegant woman. She has long, black hair and is of a pale color. She has a presence of authority that cannot be ignored.

She is a tough and direct woman. She describes her childhood as a wonderful one, full of nice memories. At an early age she was sent to work and could not study or go to school like her brothers did. My mother is the fourth oldest out of seven children.

All of my aunts and uncles have at least four children of their own as well, so you can see that I come from a very large family.

My mother tells me that my grandmother got pregnant nine times, however she lost two babies after they were born, due to sicknesses. There was not a doctor nearby that could have helped saved them. It was tragic. My grandmother was married off at age fifteen to my grandfather, who was forty at the time. My mother says he would hit her mom, and he was more like a father to her. She remembers him being loveable, a good father to them all. During the summer of 1981, while my mom was pregnant with me, her father was killed. My grandfather and one of my uncles were killed on their way home, in one day. They were ambushed and shot by a couple of men from the same town. We never knew why they were killed. When my grandmother was given the awful news, she fainted from emotion.

I sometimes think that is the reason why I am so sensitive at times. My mother says that she cried the whole pregnancy in sadness because of her loss of both father and brother. Two of my other aunts were also pregnant, and they turned out okay, so I guess I cannot use that as an excuse. I am a sensitive, caring girl that likes to cry. I find in both happy times and sad times I can just let it out and cry. I am easily put into tears when teased. That part I do not like. I want to learn to be strong like my mother and sister. They do get upset and angry at times, but they do not have the weakness I do, to start to cry. They have the ability to control their emotions and actions, unlike me. I cannot control my emotions yet. Maybe as I get a little older I will be able to control and contain myself. For me it is hard not to cry. I guess it is more difficult when one is the youngest in the family. My best friend is my sister, Helen. She is older than me, and that is why she takes care of me. She protects me from other kids or from anything she thinks might harm me. She was born with blonde hair and blue eyes, for some odd reason. As she grew, her hair and eyes got darker. She has a light complexion and does not really look like me. I have often thought that she looks like one of my favorite porcelain dolls, very beautiful. People always say that she looks like my mother and that I look like my father. I have a darker complexion and have black hair. My eyes are dark brown, and I have a round face with really big cheeks. We play all day long with each other, and we never

Me at my second birthday in Guatemala.

fight. There is no need for that. We never fight because we are the only siblings. Who would we play with if we were fighting each other? There are no other sisters or brothers around. I love her dearly.

My mother tells me that we did fight, but I do not have a single memory of that. I do not recall even one argument or confrontation, nothing. All the memories I have with her are of love. I have a memory that comes to mind, from time to time. It is of the two of us playing in the shower. She would carry me and say, "Okay, we are outside where it is raining," and we would go through the shower of droplets. She would then put me down and say, "Okay, now we are out of the rain. We are safe."

They were simple games, but to us they brought us joy. We played all day with our dolls and made up games that made us happy.

My sister and me in Guatemala.

Chapter 2

Tragedy

Today is like every other day. I have awakened; nothing is out of the ordinary. There is nothing special about it. I do not know yet that this will be the most dramatic day in all our lives. My sister and I are coloring, but my mother says we are going to wash at the laundromat. I like days that we get to go wash our clothes, because we get to leave our house. We do not own a washer and dryer at our home—we are not that rich. Where we live it is very crowded and loud. There are always people around, and every day there are parties. Our parents' friends come over, and they dance or end up fighting with each other. It is very loud when they are here, and we do not like when they come over.

We gather all our clothes that we own in the car and everyone gets settled inside it. My uncle is driving even though he is only fifteen years old. In my mind he is too young to be driving, but I guess back in Guatemala people had learned to drive at a very early age. (Louisiana does allow learner's permits to be granted to 15-year-olds.)

It is taking a long time to get there. I am not sure why. I'm looking out the window because we have not moved in a long time, and I see that we are on the railroad tracks. Our car is not moving at all. I think we are stuck. My uncle is frantically trying to get the car to drive but something is wrong. I can hear a distinct horn sound—and it's growing louder. I have heard it before from home, but never this loud. It scares me, makes me jump. I see a huge, super long train coming towards us. Could this really be happening to us? What will happen to us, will we die here? It is getting closer and closer to us. Why are we not moving out of its way! I do not understand why we don't move.

Everyone in the car starts screaming and yelling, "We are going to die!" They are all very anxious and will not stop moving—scrambling with unbuckling their seatbelts, trying to hurry. My other uncle, Chad, another of my mom's younger brothers, is sitting next to us in the back seat. He opens his door and quickly jumps out. Wow. He was very fast in getting out. Why did he do that? I cannot seem to comprehend what is about to happen to us. His shoe is stuck in the door, and he is waving his hands and screaming at the train to stop. Obviously the conductor cannot see him, however he does see us. A very bright light, yellowish-white, fills our car. It is blinding. I can feel a strong wind that is rattling the car.

Finally the inevitable impact occurs. This very large train crashes into us, and the train drags our car for a little over five miles, which to us, inside of the vehicle, feels like an eternity. The average freight train is about 1 to 1¼ miles in length (90 to 120 rail cars). When it is moving at 55 miles per hour, it can take a mile or more to stop after the locomotive engineer fully applies the emergency brakes. An eight-car passenger train moving at 80 miles per hour needs about a mile to stop. I am pretty sure this was a large train that was going at a faster speed.

All I can hear is the shrieking of the brakes from the train and the metal of our car being crushed and dragged. The grating metal sounded as if nails were being pulled across a large chalkboard. It was the most awful noise I have ever heard. We are in a green, 1976 Chevrolet Impala, which was totaled, of course, completely demolished. Every single part was of the vehicle was broken and destroyed.

My parent's Chevy weighs only about 5,000 pounds, versus the train that weighs about 6,000 *tons*. It is an extreme difference of weight, and only one will prevail in this smash up. The tires were ripped off, and all the glass instantly flew off the car and shattered. The noise of it crashing and being destroyed was excruciating. That sound will forever haunt me. It is the loudest, ugliest noise I have ever heard.

My uncle, James, my mom's youngest brother who is driving, hurts from being slammed into the stirring wheel and it breaks his jaw. He is also bleeding from hitting his chest and stomach against the stirring wheel as well. He is saying that his belly button exploded, but I do not know how that is possible. He is yelling from the pain he is in. I see tears in his eyes, and I am crying as well. My mother is in the passenger seat, and she is also covered in blood. Her back is seriously injured with a whiplash from the severe impact. Amidst the noise, she says she cannot move from the pain in her waist.

I do not know why my uncle that jumped out the car forgot to take his pregnant wife out with him. He only saved himself. He did not try to save anyone else. I know that it is our natural instinct to save ourselves. That survival instinct, that will to live, that need to get back to life again, is more powerful than any consideration of taste, decency, politeness, manners, civility. Anything. It is such a powerful force, even animal like.

My aunt is bleeding from her waist down and crying from the pain. She is eight months pregnant. The collision caused her to hit the seat very hard. The glass from the windshields is stuck in her face and she looks very scary to me.

Both my legs hurt intensely, and I cannot move them. I am trying to move them, but I can't seem to. I do not know why. I am confused.

My sister, Helen, is the most affected, from what I can see. I can see my sister lying cross the top of the seat, with all the glass from the windshield inside her opened stomach. I can see how the glass is tearing her, and I can see inside her belly. This is all so frightening. I do not know much time has passed, but I see people running to help us.

I can hear people screaming, and everything is so loud and chaotic. I hear crying, but I don't know if it is from inside the car or the strangers, it is all so hectic. People get off the train and start to run towards us to try to help in anyway they can. There are five ambulances, two fire trucks and a helicopter that come to the scene. The police and sheriff are there also. The passengers from the train are trying to help us get out of the car. One by one they manage to take us out of the vehicle and they are checking for a pulse.

Everyone inside the car seems to be asleep. This is so scary. No one is awake, and they have a lot of blood all over them. When will they wake up? I want to move, but I cannot. My legs hurt so much. I cannot stop crying. My heart is beating so fast. I cannot breathe. My eyes are closing until I fall asleep.

Chapter 3

Recovery

I wake up to bright lights and a nurse standing over me, asking me if I am okay. She asks me what my name is, how old I am, and if I know where I am. I am in the emergency room of a hospital in Bossier City, Louisiana. We were brought to the hospital closest to us. I am glad to be alive, even if I am in a lot of pain.

We were all brought in separate vehicles, each arriving very badly injured. I can hear my mother, but I cannot see her. I try to turn my head to see her, but my head hurts too much. I cannot see her. She says my eyes are open, but I cannot see her. This is so weird; I am crying from confusion. I feel so puzzled. I do not know how much time has passed. Then we are taken to our separate rooms. I am told that my sister will be next to me, once she is out of surgery.

The doctor lets my mother know that my left leg is broken—my femur bone broke. He explains that it will take several months for my legs to heal completely. I get a cast placed on both my legs, with a bar that holds them together in the middle. The doctor says that is necessary because it will be balanced that way. It is a technique they use all the time; it is just my first time encountering it. Unfortunately, it is very hard to use the bathroom. I do not like how I am feeling, this is uncomfortable. My legs itch very much, and I can't scratch them.

My aunt is having hallucinations from the fevers. She tells us that people from within the television are coming out to try to kill her. My poor aunt, I hope they can do something to stop that. I feel so badly for her. Her preborn baby had died on impact. The doctors waited five days to take her dead baby out of her body. I do not know why they waited so long. I do not understand those types of things.

I just want to see my sister. The last time I saw her she appeared dead. She was not moving. I tried reaching out to touch her, but it was useless. I was unable to. She would not open her eyes or respond. All of us were covered in cuts, bruises, and glass, but she obtained the most traumatic wounds. I do not know why it had to be her, the one most hurt. I know she is a strong girl, but I do not know if she is alive.

My uncle that was driving has his jaws wired because his face was slammed into the stirring wheel. My mother is in a wheelchair and will need to be in it for a long time. My aunt is crying over her baby that died inside of her. I am absolutely terrified to see my sister. I do not know what she is going to look like because she was covered in blood. My mother and I are in our wheelchairs, and we go see my sister in the recovery room.

The doctor tells my mother that they operated on her and were able to sew her stomach closed, however she hemorrhaged internally and is extensively damaged. She now has a scar from her chest all the way down to below her waist. They had to operate on her because her pelvis exploded, and she was bleeding non-stop from below her waist. She was extensively hurt. I can hear when the doctor is telling my mother that my sister will never walk again. She is paralyzed for life. She will never be able to have children of her own, because of the traumatic damage she had endured.

All I can see and hear is my mother crying and shaking her head. She cries and begins to pray for a miracle. My mother implores God, asking Him to have mercy and to heal her.

The nurses prepare the bed next to me, and soon

my sister and I share the same room. I am so thankful for that. I want to be close to her. My mother stays at the bedside of my sister, because she needs her more than I do. I understand that, I know that she loves me the same, but my sister's condition is far worse.

My uncle that saved himself notifies our father, and he comes to see how we are. He becomes very emotional and fearful, seeing how badly we are hurt. He was scared that we would die. There are doctors and nurses that come in to check in on us constantly. They said that I would need to have the cast on for several months and then continue getting treatment for it. The doctor says that because I am so young, I will recover faster.

My older sister is very special and has a tremendous, unusual gift. She has dreams that come true. She has always had it. For as long as I can remember, she has told us about them.

She told us that while she was asleep, a man that looked like a doctor, dressed all in white, told her He had healed her. That morning, after the dream, she awoke, sat up, got off her bed, and started to walk. She told the nurses that she was fine and could get up and walk on her own. She told them her dream, but they told her no, that she would hurt herself. They tried to restrain her, to make her stay in the bed, but she kept getting up. The doctor and nurses were upset because they did not understand how it was possible. They said it is impossible for her to be walking, that there has to be a logical reason.

It was unexplainable what had happened to her. According to science this was impossible. However, this was more than science and medicine; this was a miracle. My sister had experienced healing through spiritual power, something unnatural and incomprehensible.

My sister (left) with me in cast after the wreck.

She was up and walking and telling everyone what had happened. Of course no one would believe her. How could they? She was such a young little girl. She could be lying or making it up. I always believed her, and so did my mother. This was like nothing ever seen. Every day I like to ask my sister what she has dreamed. My sister protects me and takes care of me. I trust everything she says to me, I love her so much.

I am so happy that what the doctor had said is not coming true. She is up and walking. I want to leave the hospital already. I do not want to spend more time here. The doctor says we have to stay for a long time, until we are much better. I do not like the food or being stuck here.

Several weeks have passed, and we are finally able to leave the hospital. The doctors are concerned because they think that we do not have somewhere to live. When we crashed, we had all of our clothes in the car, and that is why they think that we lived in our car. My mother tells them, assures them that we do have a home. They still are not convinced, and they try to find programs that can help us with money and temporary housing.

Our accident was in every newspaper in Louisiana. The media was drawn to this story because a family of five Hispanics had all survived such a traumatic railroad accident. Some members of the local Baptist church found out about us from the news. They want to help us. The pastor from this Baptist church would go on a daily basis and check up on us. They never left our side. They would tell our story as a testimony of how God's hand did not allow us to die there. My mother always believed that this happened to us, first of all to bring them back to the church and secondly to serve as testimony for others. She said that sometimes people need to see God's glory in person in order to believe.

This story was being televised on all the news stations and radio stations. It was a huge headline, and people wanted to know our condition and how our recoveries were coming along. We meet a lot of new people that want to know about the accident. My mother continues to be in the wheelchair and me in my cast. Life is not so cheerful as I had remembered it. Life is different now, compared to before the accident. I cannot go outside and run anymore; I can't play how I use to.

Months have gone by, and one day my uncle removed the cast from my legs. The doctor had said that after the cast was removed, I was supposed to have a liquid inserted into my knee, but that never happened. He says it is too painful to watch me be in discomfort every day. My mom was upset because the doctor was supposed to remove the cast when I was ready, not him. He is just a teenager that thinks he is doing the right thing. I am happy to be out of it, and even though I am not healed; I am comfortable and that is all that matters. I can see the bone popped out of my left knee and that looks scary. It does not hurt, just looks funny. I think kids will be scared to play with me because of how I look.

Chapter 4

Change

The years are starting to go by, and all my sister and I ever see is my parents drinking and partying at our house. My sister and I decide to taste what they drink that makes them so happy and cheerful, and to try one of those sticks that has smoke come out of it. We hide and try to make the smoke come out of the white little stick, but we cannot. We just start to cough. We taste the drink that they all seem to love, and it is very nasty. We spit it out. We now try to put fire to a small white stick that they always have in their mouths. It tastes disgusting too. Adults like things that taste gross. Nasty, how gross, it has no flavor.

One day our dad gets arrested and is beaten up by the policemen. He stays in jail for two months and we are all sad. We miss him and do not know why he is in there. He tells my mom that he was inside of his friend's car when they got pulled over, and the police could not understand anything they said in answer, and got frustrated at them. My mother does not know what to do. In the State of Louisiana where we live, some people are mean and treat differently those who are a different color and those who speak a different language. My father is brown and speaks Spanish, so some really do not like him. Those policemen that hit my father never got in trouble for hurting him. That sort of thing happens to a lot of people and it is just the normal thing to accept. We are terrified of the police. My father did not have a weapon or anything of the sort. He is a very skinny, short man. I do not know why they felt scared of him or thought he would hurt them. I do not understand. My father is the last of five children. He was also very poor while growing up. His father died at a young age, and he only had his mother. He left to come to the United States and never spoke to his family again. It was not until he met my mother that she told him that he needed to contact them and send them money. She helped him see how important it was that he be in touch with them again.

His mother has always been so thankful to my mother for that. She says if it had not been for her, they would have never known from him again. They did not know anything about him and would worry. My dad is a great father. He has never hit us and always has a smile on his face. I have never seen him angry. When my mother gets mad at us, he defends us. He steps in, so she doesn't hit us.

Today we heard our mother crying and saying that we are moving to another state—where everything is green and full of mountains. It is a place they call the Evergreen State. We end up moving to the State of Washington. My parents sell everything we have, and we leave. It takes a long time, but we finally arrive. The way there is fun for us, because it is somewhere new to us. Washington truly is all the wonderful things that we had heard. It is beautiful, full of pine trees and very chilly. It snows here during the winter and we are intrigued. The trees and ground are white with snow and it is so blinding to see. We love it.

We met our cousins and they are the same age as us. Three girls and two boys. One of the girls, Kelly, is my sister's age. Another one, Isabel, is my age, and the other girl, Emily, is right in between all our ages. The two younger boys, Darren and Larry, are so funny. We have so many adventures together. We have fun, but also get in trouble with them. One day we found an inappropriate magazine. It was just lying there on the ground, for us to pick up. We were curious and locked ourselves in the car, to take a look at it. Our mistake was not letting the two younger boys in the car. It was just us five girls looking at it. It was like nothing we had ever seen before. Well, the two boys hurry and tell on us. Our parents come and demand we open the door and come out. We are so embarrassed and worried about what our parents will do to us.

My mother takes us home. She did not hit us. She told us it was okay to have curiosity, but that was not the way to learn about our sexuality. We never knew if my uncle hit our cousins. We never talked about what we saw, or about what our parents said or did to us. It was too shameful a conversation to have.

During this time, my parents do not drink anymore, and we are going somewhere they call a church. We enjoy going because we have lots of friends, and we learn some pretty unbelievable things. We learn for the very time about God. We are taught that Jesus loves us and we each have a purpose.

"Before I formed you in the womb I knew you; Before you were born I sanctified you; I ordained you a prophet to the nations" (Jeremiah 1:5 NKJV).

Our parents read us the Bible and teach us how to

pray. In Sunday school we are taught many things. This is the happiest and most wonderful time ever. We are learning so many things and meeting lots of new people. We are getting a little bigger and older but still play around like children. We start liking boys and start dressing a little better. We are all together with all our family. We start school and look forward to the weekends.

We love the church we go to because our cousins are there, and we have fun with them. Our parents are so different now. They never fight, and we live in a beautiful place. We had to learn another language, because at school they talk to us in English. We find it interesting that there is another word to describe or say the same thing. This church we attend is so awesome, because all the people there are so kind and friendly to each other. Every day we see them all, at different houses or parks. There are so many kids all our same ages, and we all get along. Years start going by, and we are all doing so well. Life is really great right now. We have no worries, not a care in the world. We just enjoy childhood.

My father gets a call from his boss, who tells him we have to go back to where we had lived because he has a great job for him and my mom. He wants my parents to train all of the kitchen staff, because my parents are the best workers he has had. My parents decide it is a good decision because their boss, the owner of the Superior Grill Mexican Restaurant, is paying for our trip there. He also has a place for us to live as soon as we get there. It is very sad saying goodbye to our cousins and all our friends. My sister and I don't want to leave them. It takes us five days to finally get down to Louisiana. We travel through many states, and I get carsick. I do not want to be in this car anymore. I want to be at home. My sister and I cry the whole trip because we did not want to leave our cousins. This is so awful that they can just take us wherever they decide. It is not right. I would never do that to someone I care about. Why do they want us to be sad? Do they not care how we feel or what we think?

We arrive at our new place and we are very lonely. My parents work all day and night with this new job, and it is just my sister and me all the time. We never get to see them or spend time with them, but we do have a beautiful home, we have our own rooms and lots of things to play with. It does not really matter that we each have our own room, because we are just going to play together.

Our parents' boss pays for us to go on really nice vacations. We go to amusement parks, and we get to stay at really nice hotels, but it is not enough for us. We loved being around our cousins, and we do not have friends here, in Louisiana. I wish we could see our cousins again. Months go by and we are still very sad.

Our parents have a surprise for us: we are going to spend the summer in Washington again! Yay! We are a bit nervous because we are going by ourselves. My sister is very smart. She knows everything, so I know we will make it safely. This is very fun, going back to where we were. We have a great time with our family. We have many more adventures and love their company. It is so much fun being with them. There are five of us girls that sleep in one room, so just imagine how hectic it is.

Summer is gone, and now we have to leave again to the hot, humid, lonely state that our parents took us to. Our parents are doing so well at their jobs, their boss opens another restaurant in Alabama, and my dad is sent there to train the new employees. We move into a bigger house in a very nice neighborhood. My father bought a car for my mother, for Valentine's Day. It was the sweetest thing ever. He is romantic and always does special things for her. I hope one day a guy treats me this way also.

I am in high school now, and I love it because my sister is just two grades higher than me. We go to the same school. She always takes care of me and watches out that I do not do anything bad. My sister tells me stories of how she protected me when we lived in Guatemala for a year without my mom. She explained to me that my mother left Guatemala to make a better life for us. Mom did not want to leave us, but she had to. She left us with family for a year, with her older sister, Stacy. She left and worked really hard for a year. She got a place for us to live and then went for us. We were so little that we did not know anything.

Our aunt Stacy took really good care of us. She looks just like our mom. I do not have much memory of Guatemala, only what my sister tells me about it. I was three years old then. A year later she brought us and we had the train accident. My sister says that my mother and uncles all left, leaving all of their children. They all left, leaving us in the care of my aunt who watched over us all. It was us two, all my cousins plus her children. We were eleven kids in her care. It was a full house and we always had something to eat. She is an amazing woman for taking care of all of her brothers' and sister's children. There was an older boy cousin that liked to play with us younger girls, but we did not like him because he played in a gross way. There is not much recollection of that, thankfully.

Our dad enjoys taking us to Mexico. He was born in Querétaro in the early sixties. He left his home and family when he was only 20 years old. Every year he goes to Mexico and now he takes us all as well, because he wants us to meet his mother and all his sisters and brothers. My father shows us all of the land he owns and tries to convince my mother to move there. However, she is not having it. She says it is wonderful to go visit for a week, but says she would never live there. It is funny how she said that then, and nowadays she is longing for that. She says she wants to retire and go live there.

For us it is such an adventure and we are very grateful for all that we have when we come back to our home. Mexico is beautiful and so different from where we live. They do not have what we have. The homes are made of thin sheets of wood. No one drives, walking everywhere. They prefer to walk because cars and gas are so expensive there. Mexico trades and sells all the best it has to the United States, and unfortunately their people are left with the worst of things, from food to resources.

We stop making those trips because grandma dies, and my father is too sad to keep going back. He was quite broken hearted by it. He loved her very much. My father is the youngest of his family and he was the favorite of his mother.

My parents have always set the example of what hard work means. We see in their example that they value their jobs and always go the extra mile to make sure it is done with excellence. It is undeniable that they both have traits of leadership. My parents are authentic leaders. They have strong values, are ethical, and have resilience in themselves. I am so grateful for the role models I have growing up.

My sister and I start working at a Mexican buffet restaurant, Pancho's, which is just down the road from where we live. We can only work a few hours a day because we are still in high school, and we can only do certain things because we are not 18 yet. I love working, especially because my sister is here, too. I feel like an adult now. Everyone our age has a job and gets to talk about the customers with each other.

I am earning my own money. I am so proud of my sister and I. We open our own bank accounts, and start to learn the value of money. This is so nice to have our money and to be able to spend it. We can buy things for ourselves, without having to ask our parents. Our parents do not ask us to contribute to the house, but we give them some money, from time to time. My sister is very responsible with her money. She only buys what she absolutely needs. I need to learn from her, because I want to buy everything. I hope I can learn to be smart about what I spend.

My sister learned to drive and now has her driver's license. My mother lets her drive her new car, however my sister is saving up to buy her own. We go out to eat with her friends, but only to where my parents work. They will not let us go just anywhere. My parents want to make sure we are okay and safe, but still make us think we have freedom. Sneaky.

Chapter 5

Adaptation

My sister is very smart. She is so smart that she is number two in her class, and a university that wanted her to enroll sent someone over to interview her. My sister wants to study accounting, because she is really good with numbers. She also has a passion for cosmetology. She is always fixing up my hair and trying out her ideas on me. I enjoy it because I get new hairstyles all the time. I go to school with cute new hairdo's every day. I love it. She decides to go to beauty school instead.

It is the summer of 1999, and I am so sad today. I am sad today because my sister is turning 21 and she said she is leaving. She is leaving the house. She waited until she turned 21 to be able to leave. She did not want to have my mom call the police and report her as a runaway. She wants to go and explore what is out there. My sister wants to leave Louisiana and be on her own. She told me she wants to be free to do what she wants. What am I going to do without her? She is my best friend, my confidant, my advisor, my other half. I do not want to stay here without her. I will miss her too much. Well, she makes a plan but does not tell anyone about it, not even me. She plans to leave once and for all from Baton Rouge, Louisiana. She tells me that we are going to go visit some cousins that live in Chicago. We get permission from our parents and go on the Greyhound bus, since it is not that far away. The way there is so much fun. We make stops at these interesting places. Every city had its own Greyhound bus stop, and it took us a little less than 20 hours to arrive. It was very fun for us, another adventure.

We arrive in Chicago and really like it there. It is beautiful. The city is so big. The downtown area has large, tall buildings, and there are so many people. Our family here is so nice to us. They treat us so kindly. They take us out to all the wonderful attractions, and we love it. This is nothing like Louisiana at all.

When it is time to leave and go back home, my sister lets me know that she is not returning back home with me. She buys me a pocketknife and mace so I can defend myself on the ride back. I know I will not be able to, as I am not strong like her. This is terrifying for me. I cannot stop crying, and I don't understand why this is happening. My stomach hurts.

She calls my mother and informs her of her decision. I can only hear my sister's side of the conversation, so I can only imagine what my mother is saying to her. My sister is now crying too, but she stands firm in her decision. She sends me back myself. I am in disbelief. I am in shock that this is actually happening. I am completely devastated to be by myself.

I get home. Every day I still think that she will walk through the door any time now, saying she made a mistake. It never happens though. I am lonely and feeling abandoned. I knew we would not be together forever, but I thought we wouldn't separate until later, until we were married and had families of our own. I know that life changes abruptly—it is never subtle. I talk to my sister over the phone every day, but it is not the same thing as having her here with me.

I am by myself now, and I start to rebel against my parents. I don't know who else to blame for my sister leaving. Maybe they didn't care she was gone, but I did. I was angry. I start dressing and acting differently. I am hurt.

It is the end of the school year, and I am almost done with eleventh grade. Today was a very tragic day for me. During the lunch break, in the bathroom, my best friend starts fighting another girl, for some dumb reason. My friend is getting beaten up, and I need to help her. I think to myself and decide that I am just going to pull her out from the fight. I get hit, and I defend myself. I manage to help my friend get out of that situation. In my entire school there are only two of us girls who are Spanish. There are no other Hispanic students. She is my only friend.

I pull her out and they stop fighting, thankfully. We start walking back to class. Now a group of girls are pointing to us and telling the principal that it was us who jumped and beat up the girl. It was not the truth, but that is what he heard and believed to be true.

We get taken to the principal's office. We are told that any fight that involves more than two people is an automatic expulsion from the school. I never thought I would get expelled from school. I am less than two years away from graduation. This is not fair. I am a good student and a nice person. How could I be getting kicked out of school? All I did was help my friend. I did not hit anyone.

I am more scared of what my mother will do. My mother is a very strong-willed woman. When she speaks everyone is silent, because she speaks with authority. She is a born leader and has always been in a position of authority at every job she has ever had. My mother is intimidating and never stands down to anyone. I have never known of a situation where she did not come out on top. Since my mother is a straightforward, no-nonsense type of person, she expects everyone else to be as well. Not all of us can live up those standards—especially not a teenager. At this age we are trying to figure out who we are. We have so much pressure to fit in, as it is. It is hard enough to have friends, much less be perfect all the time.

The principle calls my mom and tells her she has to come pick me up. My mother picks me up, and I have to translate what the principal is saying. Her face shows disappointment and anger all at once. I try to explain to her, but she is not listening to me. She does not care to know what happened to cause me to fight. She keeps yelling at me, telling me how I ruined my life, telling me that things would not be the same anymore.

The terrifying ride home is deathly silent. When we finally get home, she resumes screaming. She argues with all of us for days. She argues with my dad until she gives me the news that she is sending me to Guatemala.

She is sending me away because she could not

bear to take me to the center where I would need to go to complete my high school education. My friend ended up going there, and she said it was awful. There were policemen there and metal detectors everywhere. Every day there were fights. People got stabbed and cut with blades. It was a dangerous place to be. I am a little worried to go as well. I plead and ask her to let me stay. I tell her that I can work full time and help out with expenses, if she just lets me stay. I can hear my dad telling her no, not to send me, that it is a terrible idea, not to do it. He is pleading, interceding on my behalf, but it is pointless.

She is determined to make me pay for my mistake, and she sends me away. I am completely terrified, and from this moment on I start to resent my mother. It is a strong feeling. It clouds your thoughts and affects your judgment. I became numb. This was going to become a new life for me, from this is moment on.

I could not believe she was sending me to a whole other county, with people that, yes, are my family but I do not remember them—I was too young back then. How could I know who they were? I am not very sociable, and I would have to talk and socialize with them.

The flight there was fun. I got to take a connecting flight, and going through customs was fun also. I arrive at the airport, and I am just observing how poor and different it is. The smell and air are unique. The streets are very narrow, and people do not respect the lights or signs that are posted. It takes a long time to get home. It feels like hours, but I enjoy the ride.

I try to make the best of the situation. I am far away from my parents, and far from my only sister. I am alone now. I feel more abandoned than ever. Here I was in another country, with strangers. I had to keep myself in the right state of mind, or else I would lose it. I had to keep myself from breaking. I now live with my cousin, Esther, and her husband, Frank. They have two daughters, and her brother lives there also. They all are very polite and nice to me. My family here is fascinated by what they see on TV about the U.S. They ask me what it's like, and I tell them all about the food, places, houses, jobs, money, everything. They're mesmerized by it.

The food tastes so different here in Guatemala, and there is no refrigerator in their house. What if I get hungry later, what will I eat? I worry for a bit, but then I accept the fact that I am not at home and things are not the same. The house is all concrete, and it has a second floor terrace. The layout is open. It has the kitchen and living room in the same space, and the room does not have a door. The bathroom has a toilet, but we have to use a bucket to flush. I heat up water to take a shower, and then place it in a different bucket where I ladle the water out with a small pale to wash off the soap and shampoo. The bathroom does not have a door, just a curtain that can be drawn, so I only shower in the day, when I know her husband is not home. The floors are made of concrete as well, and there is no glass in the windows. So pretty much whatever the weather is outside, it is inside. The only door I see is the front door.

A garbage man comes to the door, and you give him your trash for the day. So gross! Everything else has curtains to separate each room and for the bathroom. We all sleep in the same room, but we have our own beds, so I guess it is okay. For me it is a little weird because I can hear everything. It is uncomfortable. The roof is made of sheet metal, and it is very thin, so the noise will not let me sleep. I hear the raindrops all night, and anytime there is an animal on the roof, it scares me. It is very distracting, and I just want to sleep.

When I wake up my cousin is cleaning and tells me it is time to go buy food. She takes me to the market. She warns me that the market is dangerous and tells me to be on alert at all times. She suggests that I remove my watch and secure my purse. We walk to the store and buy what she will cook that day.

The meat is hanging, and the flies are all over it. It looks gross, and takes my hunger away. When we arrive back home, her very young but oldest daughter starts cleaning the living room, dusting off the sofa and sweeping the floor. Interestingly, she does this every day.

My cousin says she is happy. She has daughters instead of sons, because they will help her out with the house chores until they are married. Her daughter is only four years old, but she is a very hardworking. When my cousin's husband comes back from work, we all eat, and then we watch television. I learn to love sports and am familiar with all the teams.

My sister sends me letters telling me how awesome it is and how much fun she having, I am happy for her. My mom calls, and she sends me money all the time. I am here to go to school, so that is what I am going to do. I am taken to school by my cousins and shown the way there and back. Her brother is my age, but for some reason he is not in school, nor does he work. However, he does take me to school and tells me to be careful. He is nice to me, but I do not like him because he does not do anything. Since he is not in school or work, he should help out at the house, with his sister. He hangs out at the corner store with his girlfriend all day long. I guess because he is youngest and a boy it is okay to do nothing.

Once I start school, I love it. I have to wear a uniform. I think this is so cool. It is a pleated, maroon and navy-blue skirt, and a white blouse. Uniforms make us equals, and we do not have to worry about what we are going to wear. The school is very different from what I'm used to. There are only two classrooms and two teachers. We are taught English, so that is an easy course to pass. I mean, I speak English better than the teacher, for heaven's sake. There is one women teacher and one male principal. That is all. Unlike Louisiana, that there are more than one thousand people per school. There are some cute boys in my class but everyone there is just friends. There are no couples.

We go on a fieldtrip to some sort of water park, and we have so much fun. A boy sits next to me and tells me he likes me. I feel flattered, but am not interested in him. I like another boy from class. Going to school is my favorite part of the day. Everyone likes me. I feel like a cool kid now. I have always been more the nerdy, unsociable, odd kid in class—never the most knowledgeable one, like here. My classmates complement me on my drawings and ask me to draw things for them. I like to draw gangsters, landscapes, people, or just letterings. They'll ask me to draw specific things for them, or I just draw from my own imagination. I remember in Louisiana I used to have my wall full of drawings and Lowrider magazine tear-outs.

My classmates seem to like that stuff too. They also really like my Old English-style handwritten calligraphy, and always ask me to write their names on their arms or just on their notebooks. It is kind of fun that they ask for something that only I can do.

One day I am invited to the movies, so I say that I have to ask permission. When I ask, my cousin's husband says no. He said they want to kill me or do something bad to me. I am upset, but I obey, of course. I was a little worried to go on the bus and then be in downtown with these youngsters that maybe did not even know what they were doing. I thought if they had given me permission it would be fun and yet a little scary. I was secretly glad he was so protective of me. He did want to be responsible for something bad happening to me. He was my guardian. The last thing I want is to get in trouble over here also. I do not go.

Later that week, they walk me home, and they are all drinking from a covered drink. They offer me a taste of it. I take a sip, because I don't want to be rude. It is the same drink I tasted as a child. I still do not like it. It was gross.

My classmates are all very nice and fun. They always hang out with each other and just listen to music and talk. I never had this in Louisiana. I start to hang out with them even on the weekend, and it is fun. Everyone lives so close to one another. I soon learn that life always changes, and things can't stay good forever.

A new girl comes to school who had recently moved from another place and transferred in. She does not like me. She says that no one should like me because I am from the United States. She insults me and is always making me feel bad. One day she tells people that she can beat me up. I do not tell my cousins or sister because I do not want them to worry.

After school the girl that does not like me, follows me home, and my classmates all follow as well. She pushes me down and starts hitting me. No one jumps in to help me. She is heavy. I cannot push her off me. I cannot grab her hands to make her stop, either. My heart is racing, and I feel like this will never come to an end. Once she has managed to hit me a few times she gets up, and then my friends help me up. I walk home very humiliated and upset. This is the most embarrassing thing that has ever happened to me, until now. I walk very slowly, with my head facing downward.

When I get home, only my cousin that does not even go to school, is there. He asks me what is wrong. I do not feel like telling him, because I know he does not really care. If he cared, he would walk me to school and back. He is only asking because he can tell something is not right. He has to be polite because we are family. I decide to tell him nothing is wrong and just go lay in my bed.

All night I replay what just happened. I think of all the things I could have done differently, but it is pointless. Why am I torturing myself this way? I can't do anything about what just happened. I must be strong and keep it together.

The next day at school is awful. The cute boy that I really liked was making fun of me. He was the last person in the world I thought would be mean to me. His brother, on the other hand, was so nice to me. He said do not worry about that girl, that she is just jealous. My close friend that I thought would have jumped in, said, "I am sorry I could not help you. I did not want to break my glasses." It was a lame excuse, but I understood her, because look where I was because I *did* jump in to help my friend. I was in now another country without my parents and sister.

The last days of school were not so great for me. I just wanted to be back home. The days go by slower than usual, and I am just counting the days until school is out. I tell my classmates that I will never forget them, and that it has been so awesome being there and getting to know them.

I finally tell my sister, one day when she calls, and she demands my parents to get me out of there. They make the arrangements, and right away I am on my way back home. I thought to myself that maybe my parents would be disappointed in me, because even in a different country I managed to get in a fight there as well. I arrived in my uniform because I wanted them to see how cute I looked in it.

My sister is recording me as I get off the airplane. I tell them all about my time there and they listen and ask questions. It is funny when I see the video; I sound so different. I have a very strong Guatemalan accent, and it sounds like I am singing when I speak. My hair grew so much over there. I do not know if it was the water or the shampoo I used, but something over there definitely made a difference. I would buy fifty cents worth of shampoo daily and use that. The money here is worth a lot more than over there. For example, a dollar here is worth 19 quetzals there. The value varies depending on the market, of course. I told my friends all about Guatemala and how wonderful it was.

All my family had the tendency to send their children off to each other's houses. I remember on different occasions my cousins coming down to live with us. One cousin's only fault was to have fallen in love with a guy. She stayed for a while, and then when she went back her brother was sent to live with us, also. I do not know why they thought this was a good idea. We would get new customs and learn different ways of doing things. Perhaps in their minds they thought it was a form of punishing us, when in fact it was exciting for us to be somewhere new. New places and new people filled with us with happiness and fun times. Each parent has their own way of disciplining their children, and I am not going to criticize how anyone does it. I know how I plan to be with my children, but it might change once I actually have them.

Chapter 6

Chaos

Now that I am back home I do not like the fact that I am by myself. I think I will leave also. I do not want to live here in Louisiana anymore, either. I decide to live with my cousins in Washington. I call one of my cousins, Emily, that lives on her own. It is summertime and I can go live with her. I tell my parents, and they are not happy, but I leave. I don't take their feelings into consideration, and I leave. I move to Washington, taking only some of my clothes. I really don't own anything.

My cousin that lives in Guatemala, the younger brother that did not go to school or work, is also coming to Washington. I bet he will feel like I did, moving to another country with very different customs. His mother lives here, and she sent for him. It will be fun to see him. I start working and going to school, but making money is more fun than studying. I work more than I study. I do not like to go to school. My cousin, Emily, her brother, Darren, and I get an apartment. We have lots of great times together. We hang out after work and meet lots of new friends.

I end up falling in love with the wrong person. He is tall, skinny, and handsome. To me he resembles Keanu Reeves. I tell him so all the time, and he just smiles. I love his smile. He is very persuasive and enchanting. The first time we went out was a surprise to me. I did not accept it because I did not know about it. He shows up to pick me up from work, without me knowing. He tells me that my cousin was unable to go for me and asked him if he could go instead. He takes me to see a beautiful view at Alki Beach, in Seattle. I love the view because I can see the Space Needle and all of Seattle.

We sit there and talk for a while, and we are having a good time. He leans forward and kisses me. I am in shock and slap him because it was unexpected and unwanted at the time. I ask him to take me home right away, and he does. He's embarrassed by the whole thing, and he keeps apologizing to me. I tell him not to do that again, that I did not want that, and he should not have assumed I did.

He shows up to the house all the time and is always calling me to talk. We talk, but I know it is wrong to be in a relationship with him, so I resist as long as I can. I begin to like his attention. We start to form a lovely friendship and enjoy each other's company. I go live with him because we are in love, and we think it is a good idea. Things are going great. We both have our jobs and are quite happy. Seems to me that we are going to make a lovely life together. Things go bad very quickly, to my surprise. I did not expect these sorts of things to happen to me, ever.

One evening we are sitting in his car talking when he makes me angry, and I kick his windshield. I storm out and upstairs to the house. He enters the house and punches me in my in one of my eyes. It really hurt. I had never been punched in my face. Never. I could not believe he had just hit me, I was scared and in utter shock. His mother is awakened and yells at him, tells him he is an animal for doing that to me. I call the police and they come quickly. I tell them what happened, and they take him away. He is arrested and taken to jail. I cannot stay to live with his mom, as she is upset with me for getting him arrested. She asks me what I am going to do now. I call my cousin, Emily, and tell her what happened. She gets ahold to our mutual girlfriend and asks her if I can move in with her, because I need a place to live. I move in with my friend, Molly. It is fine staying with her. All I have to do is watch her daughter when she goes out. Her daughter is small, so it is easy to do.

After is he released from jail (on bond) he shows up at my place of work. No one there knows what happened, so no one is startled. He asks me to forgive him, saying that it will never happen again. He said he does not know what came over him, that he is not like that, and that he has never done that to anyone before. He assures me it was a one-time thing. I truly believe him; or maybe I just want to believe him. I want to think that this was just a one-time mistake.

I go back to live with him, and things are just getting worse. He starts to insult me and tells me I am worthless, that I am dumb. He is very jealous and insecure. I do not know why he is so different now. I do not want to be in this relationship anymore. He is very troubled and has trust issues. I did not know that he would be so violent and mean to me. I feel that I deserve what he says and does to me, that it is my own fault for leaving my parents' home, for no good reason. I do not want to tell anyone. Maybe this is how everyone lives. This is my first relationship. Maybe they all start this way and end up happy. I will stay with them because he is going to change. Yet I really don't want to live like this anymore. My mom is constantly telling me to go back home, but I decide to try it out with my sister instead. I never tell my mom or my sister what is happening, I do not want them to worry about me. I decide I should leave him, and I leave to Chicago to live with my sister.

My sister is now married and lives very well. Her husband is very nice and treats her well. I live with them and start working a lot. I have three jobs now and feel exhausted. My brother-in-law does not want my sister waking me up to go to the next job; he says to let me rest. I enjoy working because I keep myself busy and out of trouble. I start to teach myself to drive in my sister's car, and I manage to save up money to buy a car. I am working and get my own apartment. However, I do not manage my money well, and I end up living at my sister's house again. My sister and husband buy a nice big house, and I get my own room.

I am happy living here and really love my sister's company. I do not know why I cannot stay still in one place. I get a call from my other cousin, Isabel, who says she is going to take me back to Washington. She says that my parents really want me back in Washington with them. She says that they own their own restaurant and could use my help. My cousin does their accounting for them. She says how well they are managing and that I should go back. She arrives and convinces me to drive with her from Chicago to Washington, just us two young ladies.

This is an insane decision. We have no idea how to change a tire or do anything mechanical. Why do we think this is a good idea? We know how to put gas in the car and drive it, and that is about all. We have a map, so I guess we will make it there. So, God intervenes, and my brand new, red Mitsubishi convertible decides to break down. Even my car did not want to make that trip with us. We end up going by airplane. Of course, my sister is upset with my decision. She tells me to really think about it. She is hurt by my decision, however she has to accept it. My father ends up flying to Chicago and bringing the car back for me. As soon as I return to Washington, I see how well my parents are doing. They have a new manufactured home, new truck, new van, and their very own restaurant, "Lopez Taqueria," located in Auburn, WA. They are really at their highest peak, or at least this is how I see it. My mother does the cooking, my father is the waiter and on weekends they have a young brother from church help serving, so they can both be cooking. I help them as soon as I get off my own job.

My parents are doing very well for themselves and assist at a good church. I live with them now and help out where I can.

My cousin, Isabel, teaches me the books, so I can do the accounting for them. She is studying accounting. I know it is tough on her to put herself through college, but she is doing it. I am so proud of her. She is the only one in our family that has gone to college, so far. She teaches me how to keep track and then do the reports to the state, how to pay quarterly taxes, how to keep personal and business expenses separate, the whole job. I am excited to be able to help them.

As soon as my ex-boyfriend heard that I was back, he starts showing up. He goes and eats at my parent's restaurant, with his friends and at times just himself. He is always around and is convincing me to start seeing him again. He tells me how much he loves me and needs me in his life. I decide to give him another chance. The mindset I had at this time was one of an innocent, young, naive girl that just wants to be loved. I believed that things could be better and that a man that hits a woman can change without any help. I think that because I love him and treat him right, one day he will reflect upon his prior actions with regret.

This time however, he is much more aggressive with me. He starts hitting me all the time and is daily putting me down, saying that I am dumb and can never do anything right. I know he loves me and will change. I really do love him very much. I know some may say that people do not change, but I know he will one day realize how wrong he is in treating me so awful. He will one day understand that this is not the way to treat someone that you love. I cannot help that I am a romantic person. I can see the good in people, even if others cannot see it.

Today I am so happy. It is the happiest day of my life. I just found out I am pregnant. He is going to be so thrilled. I told him, and he does not really know how we are going to be able to raise a baby. I know it will be difficult at first, but we can do it. This baby is part of him and me. He is still treating me bad, but I do not care because I am going to have his baby.

Why am I having this awful pain in my lower stomach? I go to the bathroom and there is so much blood. I hurry and make an appointment with my doctor, and he confirms what I feared, that I lost the baby (miscarriage).

I do not know how he is going to react. He is very violent and will say it is my fault. He will say I let this happen, somehow, that I was not being careful. I did not do anything wrong, it just happened. I am so sad and can't stop crying. I feel terrible. I do not want to tell him, but I have to.

Sure enough, he does blame me and is saying terrible things. He says I am not even good at carry a baby, that I am useless. This hurts me so much; I know that he is just angry and that is just how he is, and that is why he is saying those awful things to me.

Today his mother said something to me that really hurt. I just stayed quiet, but even my stomach hurt just from listening to her. I did not know how to respond. What could I say to her? I am the dumb one for staying with him, after everything he does. She never gets in the middle while he is hurting me. She just stays away.

We try again, and a new baby is conceived. This time I make it past the first trimester, and there is no more fear of losing it. I am so happy again, and I know that he will not hit me anymore. We are having a baby girl, how exciting. He decides her name, but I really want her to have my middle name. He will not want to hurt the baby I am carrying. Turns out he does not care that I am carrying his baby and is still violent towards me. I cry all the time, but when I think about the baby girl I am carrying I get so happy. I don't care it if insults me. This is going to be my happiest time, because there is a living being inside of me.

He is still hitting me and saying terrible things to me. I do not know why he has so much hate, and especially towards me and his own mother. When he hits me, it is very humiliating. I think he wants me to know that he will always overpower and dominate me, and for me to know I can never leave him. He always threatens that if I ever leave him, he will take my baby away. He tells me that he can leave to another county and never be found. I will never let that happen. Whenever I go shopping for food, I have to be super quick because he is counting the time it takes me to get back. If I happen to run into any kind of situation, like if there are not enough cashiers, or the checkout line is too long, and I take longer than it should take, he says that I probably was with another man. I can't talk to any female co-workers outside of work, or else he accuses me of being a lesbian. I do not know why he thinks such things about me. I just always have to reassure him that I love him. It is exhausting having to try to fill an emptiness in someone. I am completely isolated from my family. I am to never see or talk to them, because he is worried that they will convince me to leave him. This is not at all how I imagined love would be. I feel that he wants me to know he has all the power over me. It is scary knowing that my parents are so close by, just down the hill, about fifteen minutes away, yet I can't visit them. I can't even just call to see how they are, or to let them know I am okay. He is very intimidating, and I do not like it when he gets upset. He becomes violent and has so much hate inside of him. The only thing that we do not argue about is our finances. I am really wondering if this is worth it. I am not happy, but I guess it has been a long time since I truly felt happy, maybe not since childhood. I will mange to change him and he will be different towards me.

Chapter 7

Cycles

Today is his mother's birthday. I cannot wait to see how we celebrate it. We do not get to celebrate it because he has been drinking all day and night. He has not let me sleep because he is arguing with me. I need to get to work. Thank God it is just downhill, across the street, because I am too tired to drive very far. Once I get to work, and I am safe because I am away from him.

I see his car pull into the parking lot. When he gets out of the car, he can barely walk. He is completely wasted. I have no idea what he is going to do. He comes into the office and starts yelling at me for leaving the house. A Russian-speaking customer, a tall, heavy man, gets up and says, "You can't speak to her like that. Look she's almost about to have a baby."

Thankfully he is intimidated by this big man and decides to leave. However, on his way out of the parking lot he hits two cars, and then drives off. Both cars belong to customers who are in our office, watching him do so. My manager calls the police, and I am taken to the back office to talk about what was going on.

The police arrive, and we all give our statements. The owners were all there in the back office, and they told me I needed to leave that situation, that it was dangerous. They offer to give me my Christmas bonus early to help me be able to leave him. They try to make me see how bad of a situation I am in, and the danger that I am putting my unborn child in. Unfortunately, I simply cannot see it. I am weeping and exhausted from not sleeping. I never wanted anyone to know what I was enduring at home, and now everyone at work knew. It was demeaning. I tell them I will think about it. I do not tell them or the police about all the other times he has acted violently. They only know of this incident.

They see I am not convinced, so one of the owners calls my parents' restaurant. They tell my father what happened and that they do not feel I am safe where I currently live. They ask if I can go live with my parents. Of course, my father says yes, and I imagine he then tells my mom. The other owner takes me up to my house and has me take any of my belongings that I may need. I take some of clothes and leave. My boyfriend's mother is very upset with me. She tells me to think about what I am doing. She treats me like I am provoking the situation. She does not even put any blame on her son, just on me. I leave with a few things, feeling sick to my stomach with all that is going on. This should be the happiest time of my life, as I am about to have a baby. I should be treated with love and understanding.

I get to my parents' house, and they are glad to have me back. I do not talk about what just happened, and they do not ask. I do not tell them that he was hitting me. I sleep in the living room now because my cousin, Iliana from Louisiana, recently moved here to Washington, and she is staying in my old room. Her parents had sent her to live with my parents because they wanted to keep her out of trouble. It does not bother me that she has priority. I am just glad to be away from him. I can sleep in the garage if necessary. I think about other women in this same situation who do not have a wonderful family to support or help them. I am grateful that I did not end up on the streets, like so many unfortunate women do.

My mother tells me that the rule in her house is that I have to go to church with them. She says, "I do not care if you want to or not, you have to go." I hate going to church because I am ashamed. I do not want all the people there to know about my situation, and I do not want to get to know any of them. Where was God when I was getting hit for no reason? Why didn't He intervene?

Everyone there wants to pray for me. I stay in my seat during altar call, but those young ladies still go and pray for me at my chair. Goodness! As soon as the church service is over, I go straight to the car because I do not want to make friends with anyone there. I do not want to get sucked back into religion, no thank you. Over time, the preaching and teaching start to get through to me. I start taking notes at every service and begin reading the Bible. I start believing and opening my heart. One day during altar call, I prayed and asked God to come back into my life. I asked the Lord to forgive me for not protecting my unborn child as well as I should have.

I started becoming more open-minded and learning to adapt to my surroundings. I could not change anything that I had been through, only what I would let happen to me in the future. I started reading up on delivery labor because I feel like I am going to die when I have this baby. I do not know what to expect, and I am terrified. My mother assures me that I will not die from pain. However, she does tell me that I can die from losing all my blood. Goodness! That makes me feel much better. What if I bleed out? I am going to die. I need life insurance. I get a policy with large coverage amount. Because I am so young, the premium is very cheap right now. My coworkers tell me that I am now worth more dead than alive.

Today is April 26, 2002. I woke up with terrible pain in my lower back. Back when I was with him I was not permitted to go to Lamaze classes because he was jealous that I would go see guys there. I think the guys there would be with their babies' mommas, but still, those were his thoughts.

I feel like I am dying, but I do not want to bother anyone. I do not want to wake up my parents. They work so hard. They need their rest. I cannot take this pain anymore; I will wake my mom. I tell her how I am feeling, and she says yes, surely it is time for the baby to come out. She says that it is labor, and we need to head to see my doctor right away.

My doctor examines me. She says that I am dilated and that I need to head to the hospital. On the other hand, my mother decides to take me shopping at the thrift store because she knows that walking will help. I was a little worried because we weren't going, but her experience told her this was the best thing to do. I don't arrive at the hospital until six in the evening, and they tell me that they have been waiting on me. This pain is the worst I have ever experienced.

My cousin, Isabel (who helped bring me from Chicago), shows up for support. I can see her doing her homework while I am over here dying. They put me into a tub, but that is not helping. I feel like am going to die. I keep cursing at the nurses because they come and check on the baby's heartbeat every half hour. I hate the doctor because all she does is check how dilated I am and then leaves. My mother says she is going to leave if I do not stop cursing—that she is not having it. She is wearing her velo, her head covering, and she is praying for me. I don't seem to care because I am in the worst pain ever. I don't think I keep going this way.

The doctor finally says that I can push. I am excited to push because that means she is almost out. However I am concerned that I might cause a bowel movement because of the pushing. She assures me I will not and says that has only happened twice in her whole career. It is not reassuring. I start to push because I think that will be the easy part, right? No. I had never witnessed a birth myself; I only knew the gist of it. I start to push with all my strength, and the baby is not coming out. I am sweating and utterly exhausted. I have been here for 12 hours now.

My mother tells me how proud she is for me being so strong and not using any medicine to have my baby. Her words give me strength, and I push my baby out. She is so tiny and beautiful. She is placed on my chest and this is the most incredible moment I have ever experimented. At that moment I felt peace and joy.

I feel so grateful for my mother and cousin for being there with me. For a split second, I feel hurt that my baby's dad is not there with me. There is a "no contact" order in place, and he does not even know I am giving birth at this moment. I snap out of it, thankful. I am grateful for having given birth, and for not dying as I had imagined so many times. It was like nothing I could have dreamed of. My coworkers come to the hospital and meet my new baby. They brought me that day's newspaper, so I can keep it as a memory of what was going on in the world the day she was born. It was very thoughtful of them.

I can't stop looking at my baby. I do not want to close my eyes because I will stop seeing her. I guess I am supposed to know how to breastfeed her, because the nurses come in and shoves her little head on my breast. She is pulling and biting because she is hungry. This is excruciating, it does not feel good at all. A nurse gives me a nipple cover that helps me, and now I can feed her. I become dependent on it, and I freak out when I lose it.

I am able to go home. I think that because I just gave birth and the baby is out of me, that I will no longer have a huge stomach. Not true. I look like I am still pregnant. I don't understand. Why is this? My mother explains that the more I breastfeed the faster it goes away. How in the world am I supposed to take care of my baby when I feel like I've been run over by a car? This is insane. I do not know how I will do it.

According to an article in Trimester Talk, a human body can bear only up to 45 del (units) of pain, however a mother feels up to 57 del (units) of pain while giving birth, which is equal to 20 bones getting fractured.

I find it fascinating that women can withstand so much pain and yet at the precise moment we see and feel our newborn, that very same pain we thought was going to kill us is instantly forgotten. How could I have let that jerk treat me so badly when I am capable of so much strength? I tell myself that I am a strong woman, and to never forget it. My thoughts at that exact moment were of those who had just stared death in the face and defeated it. I felt invincible. It was an incredibly great feeling.

I am so tired, yet I am responsible for this living being. Every two hours I have to feed and change her. I am so tried I do not know how I will. My mother has been so incredible. She says that having a grandchild is even better than having the child. Whatever that is supposed to mean. I guess it gives grandparents a second chance. By this time in life they are much older and wiser, and have learned from their mistakes. They are usually in a better place financially and emotionally. They are able to give to and spoil their grandkids without thinking about it twice.

The pastor's wife comes to visit me. I am much too shy to try to feed my baby in front of her. I ask her to please leave so I can breastfeed. She is in shock but very polite, and she leaves. I felt badly, but it is hard enough trying to position my baby without having an audience. She probably could have helped me, but I did not think of that at the time. When you are a young, first-time mother, you are in fear of being criticized by older, experienced mothers.

One evening while home alone, when my parents were at their restaurant, my baby's father comes to the door with his mother, and they ask to come in. I let them in, and they meet his daughter, her grand-daughter. He says that he wants us to come back to live with him, that he will be a great father and will treat me right this time. His mom also speaks up and says that it will be different, that they want they want the baby with them. They ask for an opportunity to prove that they will treat the baby and me right.

I figure that it is only fair to give them the chance to prove what they say. I decide to believe them, and I call my mom to tell her that I am leaving. She is upset and says that she does not want to hear my fake, crocodile tears. She tells me to really think hard before leaving, because they want to see their grand-daughter grow up. She tells me that they know that he will not let them visit or let me come over to visit them. She implores me to stay, but I stick to my decision. I do not seem to understand how selfish I am acting. I am taking away their right to see their granddaughter grow up. I leave, and I honestly think it will be different this time around. With our new-born baby, things will have to change. I thought, he loves me because I gave birth to his daughter, he is going to treat me right. He was not at the birth, therefore he does not know what all I went through. How could he possibly be different towards me and value me for the strong woman I am?

Chapter 8

Awakening

We feel that our baby needs her own room, so we decide to buy a house. That means we both had to have two jobs. We both work very hard. He convinced his mom to stop working and to watch our baby while we both worked two jobs. We shopped for several months and finally found the perfect house, a big, three-bedroom home with two large living rooms and a huge yard. We argue from time to time, and I go and sleep at my friend's house, because I am worried he might actually kill me one of these nights. I have to leave in the middle of the night or call someone to come get us. It is very embarrassing. I cannot talk to anyone. It is my fault for being with him. I decide to take photos of my bruises, and I hide them until I am ready to report him. He ended up finding the pictures, and he ripped them up. I got in a lot of trouble for doing that.

He is starting to drink a lot again, and he finds reasons to be angry with me. I am really scared all the time, because now our baby is watching when he hits me. I need to leave him, but I have left so many times before, and each time I come back. I really need a lot of help. I am too embarrassed to ask for help. Maybe I am dumb like he says. I can't manage to get out of this situation.

My sister is coming up to visit us, and I am so excited to see her. I want to tell her what is going on, but know I will not have the courage to say anything. Maybe later I will, if it gets too hard to handle. He lets me go spend time with my sister, because he knows she will come looking for me if I do not show up. The cool thing is that my sister and I were both pregnant at the same time. Our children are almost the same age. Her son is only four months older than my daughter. Today we are all meeting up at the park, close to our home. I am worried that she might see my bruises. Last night he kicked me over and over, and now I have large bruises on both legs. I wear a long skirt to make sure no one sees the bruises. I do not want my family to worry about me. If my sister ever saw anything like that on me, she would make me leave him.

I know he will change one day, I know he will. I never lose hope of that. My sister's visit was short but wonderful. We enjoyed each other's babies. We spent a lot of quality time together. We went sightseeing all over Washington, because my brother has not seen all the beautiful scenes here.

Today I had a dream. I dreamed that I was at the bottom of an enormous hole in our backyard. In my dream I was screaming, but no one heard me. I dreamed he was at the top of hole, staring at me, and throwing the dirt back inside the hole. I felt and knew that I was going to die in there, and no one would even know that I was buried there. I saw myself climbing, using my hands and all of my strength to escape, until finally I was at the top and out. When I woke up, I knew that was it. I could feel that it was a warning of what was going to happen to me in real life. It was a time of reflection for me.

"At what point does a fly give up trying to escape through a closed window? Do its survival instincts keep it going until it is physically capable of no more, or does it eventually learn after one crash too many that there is no way out? At what point do you decide that enough is enough?"

I never knew it then, but my mother and sisters from church were praying for me. I did not learn that until later. My mother did not know how bad of a situation I was in. She just prayed for my wellbeing. My name was at the top of the list for restoration.

I interpreted the dream and accepted the fact that I needed to leave. I resolved that I would never go back to him. I am not going to die here. No, I will not let my daughter grow up without me. If in my dream I was strong, I would be strong in real life. I do not know where the strength will come from, but it will come.

I never told that dream to anyone (not until writing this). It was just for me to know. I called my mother and told her I was leaving him and that this time it is for real, no turning back. My parents are not convinced of my resolve, but that matters not. I know I am done with him.

I start to go to church with my parents, not because I want to, but because I have to. I listen to the preaching and I enjoy the songs, but I think these people are crazy. I am not like them. I do not want to become friends with them, no thank you. I am just going to do what I have to in order to get myself together. Some of the sisters are really nice to me and want me to be their friends. One lady is American, and she is really funny. We start to form a great friendship. We talk every day, and it is wonderful because we have a lot in common. We have many of the same interests and likes. I enjoy watching her growth. She truly has a great heart. She was one of my first friends, when I got my life back together.

Today I heard a word from God. He actually spoke to me. I asked God to forgive me for everything, for being a bad mother, for placing my daughter in danger, for being a bad daughter, and giving my parents so many worries and such grief. I was at the altar. There I heard God say that He forgave me. I wept tears of joy and could not contain myself. It is amazing to experience this. I can feel all of His love for me. There is a verse from the Bible that I always repeat to myself:

"The Lord will fulfill His purpose in me" (Psalm 138:8).

I had the craziest experience last night. I was sleeping in the living room with my daughter, when a very disturbing person or thing presented itself in front of me. I understood that it was a bad spirit or demon. It was hideous and didn't speak. I recognized that it was something I was struggling with, as if I had to be shown in person what I had to fight against, and now I was able to identify it and rebuke it. I did not tell anyone about this. It was too crazy to even speak of.

I now begin to engage in spiritual warfare and pray all the time. My mother and I are invited to a

Spiritual Retreat in Salem, Oregon, and we accept the invitation. Once we arrive it is like nothing we've ever experienced. We were given the rules and asked not to speak to each other about our own experiences. It is only two days, but they were two days of healing and liberation. We are instructed to imagine ourselves in our mother's womb, to remember what we heard, to remember our childhoods, to bring to memory all the suffering and hurt we had felt throughout our lives. We were given conference after conference, and the sisters giving these conferences were all so powerful, very anointed. There were two hundred women at this retreat and every single one was crying and healing. At this retreat I was able to forgive my daughter's father and my mother. I forgave and asked God to remove all the resentment I had towards them, and asked for healing in my heart and mind.

When I was back home, I wanted to keep that fire alive in me. I would make sure to keep my communication with God strong. At this point in my life, anything that I even thought would come true. I remember at work, I desired to work in a certain area, and the next day, my boss approached me and asked if I wanted to work in that area. I know it may seem like a coincidence, but they were many more incidents in which this would happen.

I am serving God now with all of my heart. I know that He has taken care of me. I know that when I would pray all those nights, asking Him to please allow me to survive through it, He was listening. Also, all those days when I promised Him I would leave this man hurting me, that He actually heard me. I am so thankful for all His love. I know that I suffered not because it was supposed to be this way, but because of my lack of assertiveness and unwillingness to leave this person that was damaging me, day in day out. I was weak minded and scared. I was in a frightened state of mind.

My ex-boyfriend and I are able to sell the house, and we each walk away with $20,000. I gave my parents $5,000 with a card telling them I was so sorry for causing them so much grief. I also buy myself a car. I keep the remaining cash in savings for a rainy day.

I decide I will continue working but also get a degree. I work and go to school and become a dental assistant. I work in insurance during the week, and on weekends I work in a dental office as an assistant. It pays the same money, so I just need to decide what I really like to do. I want to become a dental hygienist, but also have the desire to work in immigration. I start to apply to the USCIS office in Tukwila. I really can't make up my mind. I want it all.

I dedicate all my time and devote myself to raising my daughter with love. I want her to be a strong woman, unlike I have been. I want her to have the confidence to know she deserves better. I am enjoying watching my daughter grow. It is amazing how smart and special she is. When I celebrate her birthday, it is the most wonderful privilege for me. Because she was born to me at such a troubled time, I feel that she is my rose among thorns. Through hurt and pain, she was what kept me going and gave me reason to live. She is my joy and pride. There is no better time that I have lived until now.

A year has gone by, and my daughter's father came to visit me at work today. He said he no longer drank, and he was going to a church. He asked me to forgive him for how badly he treated me and said that he wanted to see his daughter and be part of her life. I told him I was going to a church as well, and that I had forgiven him.

I also told him, "If you are truly serving God, He will open doors, but as of right now you will not see her, because I do not trust you."

He said, "I am going to serve God with or without my daughter." I liked that he said that, and started to pray that God would take care of him, not because I loved him anymore, or anything of that matter, but because of his daughter. I asked God to have mercy on him and to one day permit his daughter to be proud of him. I asked for protection and guidance in his life. I blessed him and declared God's promises in his life. I want nothing but the best for him. He came around to the restaurant and spoke to my parents, telling them the same thing, that he was Christian and wanted to see his daughter. He said he was able to help financially for her private schooling and pay any medical bills she might be behind on. I welcomed the hope and let him pay for the large monthly school bill, since I had been paying it by myself for years now.

I decided to give him a chance, for my daughter's benefit. He picks her up once a week and takes her out to eat. She does not seem to be happy to go with him. I told him he needs to win her affections, and there is nothing I can do about that.

It has been several months now, and she seems to be glad when she goes with him. He takes her out to eat and they talk. It is not that great, but it is a beginning.

Today he asked me to meet him at a different parking lot, not at the restaurant like he always does. When I went to pick her up, he grabbed me and forced me to kiss him. It hurt my mouth a lot. I slapped him and left.

A few days later I told my friend at work, and she

was very wise in her response. She said, "You should go to the domestic violence advocate and tell her what happened. If she thinks it is a crime, then she will help you." I took her advice and went. I came to the advocate and told her exactly what happened. She stayed quiet, let me speak, and then she said, "If a stranger had done that to you, you would have called the police. Just because you know him does not mean it is okay. That is assault." I filed a report, and there was a "no contact" order in place. I have one of my cousins, Ed, serve him with the order.

Ed is the oldest son of my uncle that was in the car in our accident. They had four kids that are younger than us. They lived in New York for some time, then in Louisiana with us. They are such amazing young individuals. I love them so much. They have suffered like no one else, yet they are so loving. They have been through so much, yet are the most helpful, caring, amazing people I know. I am still in awe of how well they are doing, despite everything they have overcome.

This protection order I had him served with would be renewed year after year. It is a hassle to do, but I do it. It takes time to go and wait in those lines, to go from room to room on different floors. I do it because I want him to know that I do want it to happen again.

I start to really get involved in church. I am in charge of our local women's group at church, and I am enjoying it. I get lots of ideas, and I love seeing them implemented. I start to give conferences to the women and writing dramas, and I love it. I never use what I have been through, because I feel ashamed of it. I never talk about it. I keep all my business to myself and do not talk about it. I don't trust anyone with my vulnerability. I do not realize that I can help another woman in the same situation. I never talk to anyone about this ever. Not my sister, family, friends, or church members. I keep all of this inside me. It is better this way, I think. I do not want to be judged.

At work everything is going really well. I have the best job I have ever had. I have benefits and get paid more than I ever have. It is a huge blessing. My coworkers are great. They have been there since my boss started his agency, 25 years ago. My boss really likes me because I do an excellent job. When I was offered this job, I did not immediately take it, because I was comfortable were I was. I went to the interview just as a courtesy to the person that was referring me and recommending it to me. On my drive there I thought that the only way I would move was if they paid me $15 an hour. At the time I was only getting $11 an hour. When I interviewed with him, he offered me $17 an hour plus all benefits and retirement, employer sponsored. I was beside myself, but still declined. I had a loyalty to my current employer, because they had given me the opportunity to get licensed, and they paid for all of licensing and trainings. I was honest with them and told my current boss that an opportunity had presented itself, even though I was not looking. I told them what the new company was offering, and they said to give them one week to see what they could do. I called to let the new company know that I had to decline his offer, that I was loyal and could not work for him.

A week passed. My current company could not offer to cover my insurance, so I decided to get my life & disability license on my own, and then contact the new company. He is so impressed with my diligence, and he hires me. I am now able to place my daughter in a private school, and I choose the best one. With the extra money, I am able to become a U.S. citizen, and I put away the rest in savings. I am not a luxury person. I do not like fancy cars or expensive things. I like things that I can get on sale. I am raising my daughter this way as well. She needs to know that you can find good quality things, and not have to spend all of your money on it. I raise her to not be envious and to always be appreciative of what she has. I decide that when she is older, I will take her to Guatemala so that she can value the accom-

modations she has here in the United States of
America.

Chapter 9

Second Chance

Today when I walked into the church restroom, I heard two sisters speaking about me. They were saying I had brought shame to my family, for being an unwed mother and because of who her father was. You think that would have broken me, or made me resent them. Oddly it did not. It did not affect me how you think it would have. I brushed it off my shoulders and realized that there was absolutely nothing that someone could say about me that would bother me. I said to myself, if these ladies knew the brutal attacks I had received and the hell that I had lived through, they would know that simple words could not affect me. I also symbolically brushed my shoulders off to show that all of that was not important to me. It was not worth my time. I was so grateful and appreciative for being out of the situation that it seemed to me as insanity to become upset about someone talking about me. The man that I loved had verbally abused me. There is absolutely nothing that anyone can say that can affect me, ever again. I had grown from this situation and could feel it. I had gone up a level in maturity. I decided that I would never again let anything someone said affect me. I knew that I was a strong woman and that my past did not define me.

I am sure that I will never find love. What is love anyway? Love is just a decision you make, to treat someone right. Love means to respect and make one happy. To me love is not a feeling; it is an action. I do not trust a man, and I will never trust a man. This man that supposedly loved me treated me so badly, why would I ever trust a new man. I am very happy with life being just my wonderful daughter and I together. There is no need for a man in my life. The only love I desire and need is God's and my family's. I really like how I am right now. The church is really great. People there are very nice and treat me well. It is such a joy. I am so blessed in everything I have. Why change things or aspire to unknown things. I am very comfortable the way things are right now.

A couple of single guys start going to our church,

and I know they like me. They find random reasons to talk to me, and I have caught them staring at me on occasions. Today one of them actually stopped me to talk to me. He seems nice. He is always talking on his phone, at all the events that we go to. Today he called my phone and left a voicemail. He said, "Hi sister, I was just calling to say hello." When I heard the message, I was stunned that he got my phone number and called. I was not about to call him back. I said he better call until I answer him. The next day at church he didn't change into regular clothes like the rest of the men. He stayed in his suit and sat next to me to talk. It felt really nice. He asked if he could start calling me after work.

We talk on the phone every day now. He has told me all his life now. He has two sons in another state and has one brother and his mom in Mexico. He is cute and unique. Unique in the way that he is distinct from anyone I have ever met. He is so transparent and brave. I love talking to him, and we are going to start going out. My pastor and my parents say that we need to take other people out with us because we shouldn't be alone. I trust myself and know that I am not looking to get romantically involved. We go out to eat and to parks, with my daughter, of course. We have been getting to know each other for several months now.

Today he and I had to serve at a couples dinner at church. He was staring at me for a while when he asked, "How much money do we need to get married?"

I said, "What?"

He said, "Yes, I want to marry you. How much money do we need?"

I was in shock. I thought about it, prayed about it, and decided I would marry him. I had such a nice dream about him. I dreamed that he was wearing one of the shirts he always wears, a red, checkered shirt, and we were all at the park. He started giving flyers and booklets about God to all the random people he would see. In my dream or short vision, I saw all the good we could do together. As a family we could evangelize and help others know of God, with both of our testimonies we could be of great assistance to those recovering from abuse and drugs or alcohol. We would use our very tragic testimonies to help others in situations like we were in before. He spoke to my parents and to our pastor about us getting married. However, they are against it. Both my parents and pastor said that I had so much potential and he did not. On the other hand, I do see so much potential in him.

I call my sister to tell her that I want to get married, and she says no, he is not for you, you do not know anything about him, about his family. She really did not like the fact that he had left his sons in the State of Georgia. He was previously in a relationship and that did not work out. My sister said, "How is it possible for a man to leave his own blood?" I understood him because he told his version of the story, and never put himself as the victim. He took full responsibility for his wrongs and wanted to be a better person.

I accepted the challenge of becoming a blended family. I loved him and I would love his sons also. For a moment I thought that in the future he could regain custody of his children and they would live with us as well. It was a scary thought, yet I welcomed the possibility.

My father, being the wise man he is, told us to really think it through. He said you each have separate children from before this marriage you want to form. He said, "I do not want to hear later on, 'these are my children, those are yours....' Think it all through, then decide." I knew that I would love his children because they were his.

We start preparations for the wedding and looking for a place to live. I am so happy right now. My daughter likes him, and I love him. It is meant to be. It has to work. We are both grown adults that are going into this with our eyes open. We are making the decision to become a family. We are both strong spiritual people that listen to our hearts.

Today is July 18, 2009, and I am getting married. I am nervous. My sister flew in with all the family and is helping me with last minute things. My best friend is helping me with the decorations. My colors are fuchsia and brown. They are both our favorite colors. My best friend made beautiful flower arrangements for the centerpieces and for each one of our bouquets. It is a dream come true, so beautiful. I went to meet with wedding decorators, but I decide that if I am going to spend all that money, I would rather keep all my things also. I end up renting them out afterwards.

My best friend and I start looking for used items, and we just do the decorating ourselves. This is the beginning of the decorating proposition. My friend wants us to start our own decorating business. She is very excited. However, on the other hand, I do not want to. I have been proposed to start my own insurance agency at work also, but I do not want the responsibility. I do a lot at the church and I want to dedicate time to my daughter and new husband. I tell her no, and so she starts the business on her own. She is incredible at it, and outdoes herself each time. I am very proud and happy for her.

Our wedding is so beautiful. We were married at

a park outside in Puyallup. We go in our limousine to the reception in Kent. Everything is so elegant and wonderful. We have the best time ever. My sister and best friend meet and help out with the wedding. My friends and cousins are my bridesmaids, and everything is just perfect. I look beautiful in my wedding dress, and he looks so handsome in his white tuxedo. My husband and I sing a song together during the reception. Now mind you, we're not good singers, but we did it anyway. I have already prepared my daughter by telling her that I was going away for one night only. She understood it. However, some of the little girls told her, there at the wedding that I was leaving her forever. Little girls can be so cruel sometimes.

My husband's boss lent him a rental house on the beach for our honeymoon. My parents let me know that they are planning to show up to the honeymoon the day after tomorrow with the whole family. I thought she was kidding. We go to the house so he can leave his rented tuxedo and grab our suitcase, then we head out in the evening toward the ocean shore.

We end up driving all night because we get lost. I am still in my wedding dress. He wants to be the one to take it off me. All the hotels we stop at are full, because it is the Tulip Festival, which we have never heard of, and had no idea we were in the middle of it.

We eventually stay at a hotel that is very far away from where we are going, but it does not matter at this point. We have a magical night, everything I could ever imagine. Afterwards he begins to tell me very intimate, personal things about his childhood, and we are both in tears. I love him even more now, because he was able to tell me all these things that he carries with him. I guess he did not feel comfortable telling me until we were married.

My husband is such a wonderful person. He is caring, romantic, and just amazing. My parents call me and say they are there with everyone. I tell my husband, and he just laughs because he thinks I am kidding too. They show up and we all have a great time together. We all go to the beach, and they sleep there in the same house.

The honeymoon is over, and we head back to our place. We now live in a very nice new apartment overseeing lower Auburn, Washington. We do not have a dining table yet, so we eat in the living room. We sit to eat, and both my daughter and husband are sitting on each of my feet. I know that I need to give them both my undivided attention. I will make this work. I have plenty of love for them and will demonstrate to them that each one is loved unconditionally.

My daughter has her own room, and I lay with her until she is asleep. Then I leave to my bedroom.

Every night I read the same book to her. I want her to know it by heart. It is a kid version of the Bible. Everything is so special right now; I cannot believe I have my very own little beautiful family. It is marvelous to have so much love both from my daughter and husband.

Chapter 10

Detachment

Today my mother came and just started putting all of my daughter's clothing and things into a bag and telling her that she was staying with them now. This is inconceivable. How can it be? I cannot believe this is happening. I do not understand it. I ask my mom what she is doing and why, and she just repeats the same thing other and over. I am crying as I see my daughter with her eyes wide open, just going along with this. This is the most bizarre thing that has happened. Did my daughter ask to live with them, and I just don't know? I find out later in life that my daughter did say that she was lonely there at our new apartment, and that is why my mother took it upon herself to make her happy. Now my daughter's room is there, but she is not.

Telling my husband what happened was weird, because I did not comprehend it either. I told my mother that my daughter needed to stay there, that this is her home now. He was upset and said it is not right. But what could he do? He just saw how miserable I was and was hurting with me. There is no fighting with my mother. She gets what she wants. My mother is confrontational and sees life in a different way than I do. It is a rare occasion that we see eye to eye on things. I like to see the good in everything and everyone, and she on the other hand, thinks with reason and tries to evaluate each situation.

I am very sad, and now I am feeling a pain in my shoulder. I need to go to the hospital. I go to see the doctor, and he gives me the surprising news that I am pregnant. We decide not to tell anyone until I am further along. My husband is so anxious he tells his cousin right away. Weeks have gone by, and I am not feeling so well. I use the bathroom, and I can see a large bloodworm-like figure in the toilet. I leave work immediately and go to the emergency room. I wait in that room for hours. They do not seem to care the pain in I am in. I call my husband to tell him, and then I call my mom to let her know I was not going to church that evening. It is infrequent that I am not at church. I always attend.

The doctor confirmed that I had lost the baby. I was completely devastated. I could not believe this was happening again. The only person I called to tell was my sister. I did not want to tell my mom, not even my best friend. I cried all night. My husband was so supportive and incredible, nothing like my previous miscarriage. I manage to overcome it through prayer and support. I kneeled down by my bed and thanked God. I told him that I was thankful for the amazing husband I had, for being so understanding and loving me.

I told God I do not know why this happened but that I trusted Him in everything. God knows what He is doing at all times and has everything under control.

"So do not fear, for I am with you; do not be dismayed, for I am your God. I will strengthen you and help you; I will uphold you with my righteous right hand" *(Isaiah 41:10).*

My mother-in-law is diagnosed with ovarian cancer, and she is not doing well. She is very sick and is suffering. This sickness is tearing my husband apart. He tells me everything that his mother suffered throughout her life. He cries as he's telling me all the horrendous things his father would do to her. He tells me in detail the beatings and rapes his mother endured. He lets me know how his father almost killed him on occasions and how he loves him very much, despite the violence towards him. My husband's father died of alcohol overdose.

Even after his father died, his mother continued to suffer. He tells me that he never understood until he was older all the sacrifices that she made for him. He feels impotent, powerless, having to see her in pain and not being able to take it away. He talks to her every day and sends money for her treatments. In Mexico you cannot receive services and then pay, like we do here. If we go to see a doctor, we have the option of being billed and paying later. My husband works extra hours and is able to send her money every week. In March of 2010 my husband gets a call saying she is doing very badly and is unresponsive. We know what is next.

The following day, on Sunday, we are at church when my husband receives a call. He starts weeping at the news that his mother died. He tells our pastor and the pastor passes the microphone to him and he informs the congregation of what happened. The congregation takes up an offering because he is flying out the very next day to Mexico. He wants to bury his mother. We go home and start looking for flights. We find a flight for the exact amount that was raised for him at church, $637. I can see God's hand in this.

My husband talks to my parents and asks them to

please watch over me while he is away. They assure him that I will always be watched over. I know that I will always have food and a roof with them.

I take my husband to the airport, and he leaves me specific instructions on what to do in case something happens to him at the border. He is going to cross back into the United States illegally, and it is very dangerous to do. All the stories my mother ever told me came to mind, but I know it will be even more difficult now. Times have changed and people only get more dangerous in advancements of weapons and detection of illegal entry. I pray that he makes it there and back safely.

My husband has been away for couple months now, and it worries me that he has not been able to cross back over. I am so sad, because not even my daughter is with me. I feel very lonely. Since my parents took care of her while I worked, she formed such a great bond with them. To her they are her parents, not me.

I understood at this moment that possibly I would have not handled the pregnancy well, and that this was the reason it happened. Everything in life has a purpose. I pray for him every day, all day long. I know God will protect him and bring him back. The brothers and sisters at church are so supportive and encouraging. I am so grateful for them. They bring me groceries and tell me that they are praying for him also. I am glad I am able to speak with him every day, so I know that he is safe. He tells me all about how things are over there, in his home in Mexico.

It is May of 2010, and he said he was finally able to cross, and he is on this side of the border. However, he needs to pay $3,000. I do not know what to do, because we do not have that money right now. We have not saved up any money. Lord, help me think of the person that is going to be able to help us out. The person that comes to my mind is my boss. He will be able to help us. I am going to ask him. I go to work, and I ask my boss for an advance on my pay. I was completely honest with him and told him the situation. He was very understanding, and gave me the money, in cash, at that very moment. He said he would deduct $500 from my paycheck in each pay period. I am so grateful to him for doing that.

I was able to speak with my husband, and followed his direction on how to get the money to the right place. Once the money is paid, he arranges a place for me to pick him up. He told me that unless I heard his voice, never to deposit money to anyone. So, I made sure it was him and not a scammer trying to get money from me. He tells me that we have to have a code message to know it is each other on the line. I am going to ask my cousin, Isabel, the one that went for me in Chicago to go with me when I go for him. She is thrilled to go, because it is always an adventure when I am with her.

One time we were in Texas with her, and we went on a church crusade. It was such an awesome time. She is quite a traveler and very intelligent. My cousin is a great role model for any young girl to follow. She's studying and working to become a better person. My parents let me use their credit card to pay for whatever I may need along the way, especially for the gas to get there and back. I drive for 24 hours straight. I do not let my cousin help me drive. I just need her company to stay awake.

My cousin and I arrive in California and spend the night there, because we need to rest before coming back home. My husband is so skinny and dark skinned. He looks so different physically, not like the same man I married. We spend another magical and unforgettable night together. It feels so special to have him here again with me. He tells me all about his adventure, and I am filled with tears listening to his horrific experiences. He tells me of people that actually died, of people that could not make it back. He had crossed several times before, so he was prepared yet still suffered.

I cannot drive even five minutes on the way back, so my cousin and husband take turns driving back home. It is a wonderful trip, and I am beside myself to once again be united with him. We arrive at our apartment, and it seems so unreal that he is here again. He is a different person though. I do not know how to explain it, but he has changed. I try to understand that he is grieving and will go through all the different stages of it. He is really hurt, but he is strong. He told me about an interesting dream he had. He said in his dream, our church was destroyed. The building had collapsed, however, there were four columns that were being held up by members of the church. In this dream, he said God told him that it would collapse, but to stay firm and strong. He gave testimony at the church in California and at ours. He did not understand it, but said he would obey.

I am thrilled because he has only been back a week but he has a job already. He is working at a small burger restaurant. He is the cook. He brings me food every night. I love him. He wants to work where he was before, doing construction. He says he does not like being locked inside the kitchen all day, seven days a week. He wants to be outside, painting and doing manual labor. I wish he would stay indoors because it is safer, and it is a steady, reliable job. When he works construction, they can only work in good weather. I want him to be happy, and he is not right now, there where he works. He starts at the construction job once again, and it bothers me because some days he has to stay home.

Today I decide to tell my daughter about her father. She is eight years old, so I figure she can understand now, so I decide to explain to her. I tell her that I do not want people that do not like me, or do not like my parents, to come and tell her. I tell her that people will want to tell her about it in a hurtful way, and I rather tell her myself. I explain to her that we were very much in love and did not care what people thought. I told her we hurt both our mothers in the process, and that they were both very upset with the whole situation. Like any good mothers, they decided to accept and adapt to the circumstances. When I had our daughter, it just joined us all. She was the reason that our mothers were speaking to each other.

When I told my daughter, she said she already knew. She said a cousin of ours had told her already, and she was confused. I explained to her that she had to be born, that she had been born with a purpose and a tremendous ministry, that we both loved her very much, and that she needed to be strong and not resent us for it.

I told her that we were talking it out so she would know. My greatest fear has always been that when she found out, she would rebel against us. It was something strange to accept.

For his mother, it did not matter. She would tell us to try to be happy because was not able to choose the man she wanted to be with. You see, the man that wanted to be with her took her out of her home at gunpoint. Her father could not do anything because it was seven men that came in with guns. Days after she was taken, the man came and talked to her father saying that he was going to marry her. She said she liked her boyfriend at the time, but this other man stole her. She talks about how much she suffered and does not wish that on anyone. She would tell us that we could be happy if we wanted to be together.

Chapter 11

Trusting God

My husband speaks with me with such love and understanding. He suggests that I let my daughter's father back into her life. He says that I am a Christian woman and that I need to forgive and allow him to see his daughter. He tells me that it is not my daughter's fault how he treated me, and that I needed to look past that and give him the opportunity to start a relationship with her. We talk for days on this until he convinces me. I never tell me husband all the awful things I went through. For me it is shameful and not important for him to know. I call her dad and give him the great news, that he is able to see his daughter again. He is very grateful and sounds so happy. He starts to see her again. I let him know he should be thankful to my husband for intervening for him, and he is in awe.

I go to the doctor because I am not feeling well, and I am given the news that I am pregnant. Wow, this is such great news. I am filled with so much joy. We are going to have a baby! My husband is so happy, and we are ecstatic with excitement. We are having a baby boy. I was secretly hoping they would be twins. I didn't know what I was asking for. Imagine two boys the same age. Wow.

I get a crazy idea; I am known for those. I get an idea in my head that we need a bigger place, and the baby he needs his own room, which he really would not need until later when he was more grown. My husband is excited about the idea, because he wants to be able to paint and do projects to his own home. We start to shop for a place of our own, and we find a mobile home for only $20,000. We buy it and move in during the very last month of my pregnancy. The timing was not a good idea. I am uncomfortable and can barely get around. We start to paint and fix up our rooms. This is all so exciting.

Today I woke up with a lot of pain in my lower back. I know this feeling. These are labor pains. I call my husband, and he leaves work to meet me at the hospital. I call mother to please take my daughter to school and take me to the hospital. We arrive at the hospital, and the pain is much stronger. I feel like I am going to die. My mother does not want to leave until she knows how dilated I am. My daughter keeps going to the bathroom because she is nervous from seeing me in so much pain and screaming. She is too young to know what labor is. I tell my mother I am too old to be having a baby and that I will not make it this time. We have only been here an hour, but my baby is ready to come out. The doctor says it is time to start pushing, and he comes out very quickly. One push and he was out. I cannot believe how quickly it was. Thank God I had arrived when I did, or he would have been born at the house.

This is so different from my daughter's birth. It was a much faster labor. I am completely dilated within an hour of arriving. My mother did not get a chance to leave and come back. She happens to pull the curtain open and my nine-year-old daughter got to see the birth. How awful. My daughter tells me it is the grossest thing she has ever seen. Maybe this image will stay in her mind and help her not have sex before it is the right time.

All our friends and family come meet our new-born son. I get to see all my family and friends that I do not usually see. We have lost touch because we all have our lives with our children, and we live for them now.

Things are so wonderful right now. My husband is so amazing. He feeds the baby, sleeps with him, takes such good care of him. I am so blessed with him. He tells me that this is his chance to be a better father. My daughter is learning how to be a big sister. She plays with her little brother. She loves him a lot. She lays him with all her dolls around him. It is very cute to watch.

Two weeks have gone by, and I need to go pick up my paycheck. I can show my baby to my boss and coworkers. Everyone at the office is so cold and inattentive to me. This is weird. They are my friends, and I thought they wanted to see my new baby and me. I mean these are the same wonderful ladies that surprised me with a baby shower right before I had him, so why are they acting like this with us? My boss gives me a huge bonus and is always telling me how I am doing a great job. I love my job; this is the best job I have ever had. My boss is not there. I am told that he will call me, so I leave. I sense things are not good. On my way back home, I get a call from my boss. He tells me that I need to find another job. He says I need to take the three months of paid time I have to find somewhere else to work. I am in shock. He does not give me a reason for doing this. I have a sinking feeling in my stomach, and I feel like I am going to throw up. I get in the car and tell my husband what happened. I cannot stop crying. I don't understand why he is doing this. My boss had a tendency of firing people for no reason, but I never thought it would happen to me. I really did think I was special. I was making him so much money. I was bringing in all the new business for him. All the other ladies had been with him from the start, but they were only serving the clients. I was the one bringing in the Hispanic market. I would get there early and eat my lunch at my desk, because I did not want to stop working. I would leave late. I was so grateful for this job. I did only my very best every day to help grow his business. I would pray every day for the success of my boss and coworkers. I remember talking with the other ladies, asking them why he had not fired me yet. They said, "He really likes you; you made an impression on him that he cannot forget." I felt so special. It really boosted my self esteem to hear that.

My husband looks at me through the driver's rearview mirror, and tells me to take a look at our son, and to accept it and see it as a good thing. He tells me that this way I will be able to spend good quality time with our baby. I am still uneasy, but I start to think that everything that has ever happened to me has always had a reason, an importance to it.

This was the first time in my life I was without a job. I have been working since I was 15 years old. It was such an uneasy feeling, having to depend on just my husband's income. I felt stressed, angry, and hurt all at the same time.

Within a week of my firing, I receive a call from my boss's competitor, and he offers me a job. I go and meet with him, but the pay is a five-dollar cut from where I was. Of course I decline. A week later he calls me and says he cannot pay me more than what he offered me, but he can let me work from home. It is exactly what I need. I accepted the offer and made money while being able to stay at home with my newborn. I am making sales and working internet leads.

Almost a year has gone by when my husband makes a comment about me eating a lot and acting the same way as when I was pregnant. I laugh, but I still take the test, and yes, I am pregnant again. This time I am having a girl. It is awesome that my oldest daughter will now have both a brother and a sister. How awesome, two girls and a boy. So great.

We are thrilled, and we start to make preparations again. My oldest daughter lives with us once again, and that makes me so joyful. I have a wonderful, great little family again.

It is August and the hottest summer I can remember. I am so uncomfortable, and I am ready to have this baby. I try doing home remedies to provoke this labor, but nothing is helping. Finally, she is ready to come out. It is Sunday morning, and I am in labor. We head to the hospital, and I am prepared. She takes a long time to come out, just like my other daughter. However, this time I have my music playing trying to relax me. I hear the song Healer (by Hillsong) over and over, and it is smoothing. I think that girls are harder to give birth to, or at least it is in my personal experience.

Eight hours go by and I can finally begin to push. I push and I push but she is not coming out. I turn to see my husband because he is no longer by my side since I keep digging my very long nails into him. I turn to see where he is, and he is knocked out, snoring super loud on the small couch that is there. The nurses also see him and ask if he needs medicine or if he is okay. I tell them do not worry about him, worry about me!

I do not have any strength left and feel like I cannot do it anymore. I push out really hard, with all of my strength, and I force her to come out. She came out with a bruise on her face. She looks just like my sister, but my husband says she looks like his family. All of our friends and family come to see her. I am so happy.

My husband is starting to miss a lot of church, and he is never at our church functions. This is getting frustrating. I do not fight with him; I just pray that God can make everything how it was before. He is working a lot, but I do not see more money coming in. Something is wrong here.

On one occasion we talked, and I asked him to tell me what was going on. He said something to me that made me think. He said, "If I were drowning, would you not jump in the water to save me?"

He surprised me by that question, but I quickly answered him, "There is no reason for you to be drowning. You have a lifejacket on (God). Take a look your surroundings, snap out of it, and get it together."

He did not like that response. I tried to be understanding. I did not know what he was going through, and he would not talk to me about it. I do not think he trusted me to tell me. I hated to be so tough on him, but that is what I felt to say.

Life is complicated. It is not a fairytale or a happily-ever-after. I have learned so much in these 30 years when I have been stuck in situations that I did not even know how I got there. I remember on occasions where I did not make the best decisions. Once time I had to fight off a guy that was trying to have relations with me. I remember using all my strength and getting bruised up until I was able to escape. I remember being so angry with my friend for setting that up. It took me a long time to be able to forgive her, but I eventually did. I remember that one weekend my boyfriend and I drove to Ellensburg to take my cousin to see her boyfriend, and she disappeared the moment we arrived at the fair. Our car would not start, and she would not answer her phone. My boyfriend and I asked for help, but since the car alarm was going off, people did not want to help us. Maybe they thought it was stolen, and that is why they did not want to help us. Who knows? We ended having to push the car out of the fairgrounds, and a young guy saw us and approached us. He invited us to say at his house. He was our same age, and said he understood us.

So, here we were having to sleep on a stranger's sofa until morning, telling this stranger's parents we were all friends from school. Thank goodness they were good people. Who does that—sleep in a stranger's home? There were a lot of unsafe, crazy decisions that I can look back on now, and just wonder what I was thinking.

I am happy to actually think carefully before I do something nowadays. I try to see things from all the different angles and outcomes. I have a much better perspective on life now. I have the ability to not only see the bad but also the good in the situations we are placed in.

"All things are subject to interpretation. Whichever interpretation prevails at a given time is a function of power and not truth." –Friedrich Nietzsche

Our neighbor does not like us, and one night calls a tow truck on my vehicle that is parked on our property, however, in front of our home not in our carport. The neighbor on the other side of our house comes and knocks at our door to wake us up and tell us. I see the tow truck driver hook up my car. I go out there, and I am arguing with him, asking him why the other vehicles in the same situation, are not being towed. He says this is the only car that we got a call on, and he cannot just go picking up cars, there must be an order for it. The tow truck driver tells me to take it up with the manager. I cry all night because I am upset, mostly at myself. I am mad at myself for not having the $500 and some odd dollars to just pay the man to unhook my car. How is it possible that I do not have the money in my account to pay? This is ridiculous. I am also upset at the neighbor for calling, at the tow truck driver for doing his job, upset at everyone.

The next morning, I come up with the money and try to pick up my car. When I arrive, I am informed that the tow truck driver was lifting my car to place it down, and it fell off the lift. I am in shock and I immediately start to cry. I am crying because now I will need a new car. I am already very emotional. Then I ask who is going to pay, and he says that in 25 years of towing cars, this has never happened. The tears stop, and I ask how much money are they paying for my car? The funny thing is that I had been trying to sell my very old Chevy Blazer for more than a year. It was in very bad condition. Every day I would pray that I would make it back home in it safely. They end up giving me more than $4,000 for it. My car was worth less than $900 in Kelly Blue Book price.

When I call to tell my husband what just happened, he cannot believe it either. He laughs and tells me that I must have arranged that. He asked me who I told to do that. He is crazy. I tell him that I know that God was the one that made this happen. It was a test of faith in God. I needed to learn once again, that everything is under His control and that He allows our pain for his glory. Romans 5:3-5 says,

"Not only so, but we also glory in our sufferings, because we know that suffering produces perseverance; perseverance, character; and character, hope. And hope does not put us to shame, because God's love has been poured out into our hearts through the Holy Spirit, who has been given to us."

With the money they give me, the kids and I take a trip to go see my sister, in Chicago. My husband could not go because of work. We have a great time there for a week, and I can see that God helped me in this situation.

What people with bad intention use to hurt you, God turns around and blesses you with the very same thing. It is true that God works in mysterious ways.

An opportunity presents itself of me starting my own business. I have been in the same industry for 15 years now, and I want to believe in myself that I can do it. I pray and talk to my husband about it, and he is on board. He wants me to succeed. I reflect on all the success I have had in sales, and a great desire to succeed is born. I take the risk and open my own insurance agency. From a standpoint of startup cost, I research and consider all the different insurance companies out there that an agency can be affiliated with, and I settle on one. It takes a lot of work to start a business. First of all, you need some money, which I do not have, but I know I can make it. When it is your own business you desire for everything to turn out smoothly and great. Not so in my case. Customers are very demanding. This was something I already knew, but previously I was able to leave at 6:00 PM and not worry about it. Now that my name is on the door, I can never stop worrying about it. This is stressful. Everything is awesome in my first year. It is incredible to be making good money. Some people that I knew actually support my business while others do not even return my calls. I thought everyone would be running to give me their business, not just because it was a great company, but also because they wanted to bless me. That was not the case.

I felt hurt but understood that some people are not happy when you succeed. They are happy for you just as long as you are under or next to them at the same level. The moment you exceed them they will not like you anymore. There are certain jealousies that arise in some people, and I have never understood that. I just make sure I am teaching my children that they need to be happy for their friends and celebrate the victories of others. I have always been so happy to see my friends succeed. I wish them well, and if they ask for my business, I give it to them.

There needs to be a genuine sense of gladness in seeing others become successful.

My second year in the business, however, is not so good. Things seem to go downhill until everything is gone. I know that life is like this, with ups and downs. We need to enjoy the top and be stay humble because we'll be at the bottom at times. We all have our good, amazing days, weeks, even years, and then we have our days, weeks, and years that are just plain awful.

"I ask two things from you, Lord. Don't refuse me before I die. Keep me from lying and being dishonest. And don't make me either rich or poor; just give me enough food for each day. If I have too much, I might reject you and say, 'I don't know the Lord.' If I am poor, I might steal and disgrace the name of my God" (Proverbs 30:7-9).

Around this same time, my parents were offered and given a church in Sumner, Washington. The current pastor had to leave for Puerto Rico. My father is a pastor's assistant, and he does a great job, according to the members.

On a Sunday at our local church, instead of our regular service, we have a large going-away party for my parents. Everything is just so nice. Our pastor asks me be in charge of it, and I do a great job at it. I decorate and get the food organized. Everyone speaks and declares blessings over them. It is such a beautiful event. My husband and I decide to stay at the local church because we both are in leadership.

A month after they leave, there is a disaster at church, and it begins to fall apart. The worst thing imaginable happens. Our pastor is found in adultery, and he is removed from his position. Our church was now without a leader. Many members left because they were outraged. I stood firm because while what happened was terrible, the pastor was not God. Although it made me think that if such a good Christian, our leader, our counselor, had betrayed his wife, what could we except from our husbands? It really made you think. **My relationship is with God, not with man.**

My husband was deeply hurt. He felt betrayed, and could not believe that such a great, God-fearing man had fallen so low. It was hard to go to church, but we did it. A new minister came and was assigned to be our pastor. He has a big beautiful family, and he starts to rebuild from the destruction. It was difficult because the members were very discomforted. We become good friends with this new family. They are wonderful people, a God-fearing, strong, loveable, hard-working family.

I write about this because it was something sinful that only two people did, however it affected several hundreds of people. Many people were wounded and lost their trust and faith in God.

It was a very dramatic point in all our lives. People kept calling my parents to ask if they knew. Of course, they did not know. They loved our pastor and his wife immensely. He was their spiritual son and they watched how he grew in ministry and maturity. I remember all the tears and words of comfort they tried to provide to every one that would call them, looking for answers and hope. My parents visited and talked to our pastor and wife. It seemed there was just too much damage to fix.

The only two solutions there were in this case were to separate and never look back, or to forgive and stay together. She chose the latter, and to this day they are still together. She said she did it for her children. I remember we were all invited to hear a conference given by her, and it was very inspiring. She spoke of how she did not understand why she had to go through that, and why no one was there with her, during it. She said that she understood there are some things you have to pass through *by yourself*. A couple of years of ago, I remember being invited and going to their daughter's Quinceañera (15th birthday). It was very wonderful to see them again. They helped my husband and everyone I know, so much.

Chapter 12

Devastation

I get a call from one of the sisters from church crying and telling me that someone from church has been molesting her daughter. She tells me to ask my daughter if this man has done anything to her. My stomach drops to the floor because a memory comes to mind immediately. The prior week we had a couple's event at church, and I asked my daughter if she wanted to stay at her friend's house as her uncle would be the adult watching them. She had a face of terror and said no. I did not pay too much attention to it, and said, "Okay, I think your dad's mom can watch you," and she was relieved. Her grandmother ended up watching her that night.

I go to pick my daughter from school, and I ask her if that man had ever touched her. She immediately starts to cry, but says no, he has not touched her. I tell her there is nothing to be ashamed of and that this is the time to speak up about it. She says no again, however, she is still crying. I call the sister back and tell her my daughter said no.

My daughter spends a week locked in her room. She doesn't come out to eat with us or anything. She finally comes out and tells me that yes, he had been touching her as well. I decide not to call the sister, but to inform the authorities right away. We go and make a police report, and he is arrested. His boss pays the $10,000 bail and gets him out immediately.

The trial begins, and we attend on every single court date. It is dreadful to walk into the courtroom and have to deal with this. His lawyer uses the lamest strategy to get him off. He states that he does not speak Spanish and they have been unable to find a translator that speaks his dialect. It is absurd, so I give them proof that he graduated from our Bible college and that he could not have done so without speaking and writing Spanish.

I have to tell you that guilt is the worst feeling ever. Guilt exceeds hate, love, or any other strong feeling. I was overwhelmed with guilt. This awful thing had happened to my daughter while I was serving in my church—while I was selling food and raising funds for charity. This was happening while I was worshipping God, while I was in a living sacrifice of fasting and in daily Bible devotionals—while I was in the deepest, constant communication with God and feeling His presence. This is all too much to understand. I do not blame God for allowing it. I blame myself for not knowing about it. I cannot sleep at nights. I cannot stop thinking about it and replaying it in my mind. I cannot be intimate with my husband, taking pleasure and knowing that my daughter had to be exposed to such things.

My husband is so caring and sympathetic. He gets up and starts to pray for me. I can hear him asking God to comfort me and to give us all strength for this process. I am so thankful for such a terrific partner. He is amazing. He takes the time to write notes to us and leaves them on the fridge for us to read before we leave each day.

The trial finally begins, almost a year later. We are notified to go. My daughter testifies, I testify, the other young girl testifies. Overall, this procedure takes over two years. It is exhausting having to wait on the justice system. Will justice prevail, and will he pay for what he has done? I honestly do not know.

I had a nightmare last night that this creep actually cut off the head of the judge, and that the bailiffs said they couldn't do anything to him. Then, today they said it was a hung jury. My daughter is completely devastated. I am so upset because they are unable to bring him to justice. There is no justice for us. I cannot do anything but watch her feel helpless and vulnerable.

A month later, on a Saturday morning, my daughter and I are on our way to see the venue for her Quinceañera, and we are stopped at a traffic light, when—of all the people on earth— we see him crossing the street. He looks at us both, and we do not say anything or even acknowledge that we saw him.

We see the beautiful venue, Victorian Gardens in Kent, and go back home. On Monday, at school, my daughter has a panic attack, and my mother goes and picks her up. My mother leaves her at the house while she goes and runs errands. When I get home from work my daughter tells me that she had such an amazing experience. She tells me that she cried and prayed to God, setting this horrible man free. She said that he was out and free to do what he wanted, and she questioned why was she going to be suffering. She forgave him and placed him in God's hands. She said she let him go. I felt so proud of her. I was still not able to forgive. I kept saying to myself, if she has done it then so can I. It just was not in me to do. It was too painful.

The worst feeling in the world, is when you see your children in pain and you aren't able to take away their pain.

Surprisingly, that same week on Friday, he gets into a terrible accident at work. I get a call from his co-worker that also attends our church, stating that this man had been in an accident. He was thrown from a machine at work, hurting his spinal cord. He had broken ribs, and he had badly injured his head. I immediately called the prosecutor and told her that if they call him now that he would confess. I was sure of it, because he was in physical pain. He would be so vulnerable that he would own up to what he had done. Sure enough, the prosecutor got ahold to him at the hospital and he said yes, he would plead guilty. We were relieved.

However, because of technicalities, his lawyer argued that because he now had a brain injury, he would not be competent to stand before a judge. Another year and half go by until he is, finally, able to accept his sentencing. We are notified the day before, and we are asked if we want to speak. My daughter is hesitant because she does not want to see all his family there. It will be difficult. Her best friend used to be his niece, and it was so painful when another girl that had been abused told my daughter that it was her fault. This other girl told her that if she, my daughter, had spoken up, it would not have happened to her. My daughter felt guilty, and I had blamed so many different people for this also. In the end all we can do is forgive. It is probably the most difficult thing in the world to do. It took me an extremely long time to forgive all these people.

When we arrive at the sentencing, there is not a single person there to support him, and we are all glad. I thought that his brother would be there for support, but he was not.

Prior to this, his brother had the indecency to call a meeting at church with all the ministers and their wives. He said the reason for his meeting was to say how upset he was with us, my husband and I, for preventing his brother from attending his niece's Quinceañera, which was at our church. There was a protection order in place, and that blocked him from coming near my daughter. I had made sure he was legally served the order, and sent a message with the same person serving it, that he was in no way permitted to attend. His brother said that the other sister had the decency to tell him that they had filed charges against him. I could not believe he was calling us out in front of everyone. I got up and left to the kitchen. My daughter was not in the meeting, but she knew what it was about because it was her best friend's father who had called the meeting. After a few minutes of gathering my thoughts, I pulled myself together and went back into the sanctuary, where the meeting was taking place. I sat back down and continued listening.

My husband got up and said, "How can you possibly think that she is lying? How could she get up there and play the piano and sing, how could God use her, how could she have so much anointing? She is not lying!" After hearing him I got the courage, and I got up to speak. I wanted to ask him, who in God's name told him to do this meeting? It was most humiliating to my daughter who was not in the meeting, and it was putting all our business out there for people who were not involved and did not need to know our business. However, all I could say were hurtful things. Hate came out instead of reason and logic. I talked about how his brother was. I talked about the fact that he, the person that had called for the meeting, had been arrested for picking up a prostitute. I asked him, how would we possibly know that, if it had not been for his brother that told people all about it. He then proceeded to defend himself, saying that he did not know she was undercover, that it was a set up. I said in front of everyone, that is what you say, but my point is that you are defending him when you do not know what he is capable of. I know that we will always defend our family, above all.

Each minister spoke. I loved that none of them sided with him. To this day I feel like one of the ministers had advised him to do it that way. I guess I will never know.

This was the day her dad found out about the whole situation as well. He saw her so upset and of course she told him. He came over to the house after church and we talked about it. I explained that we had taken all the necessary steps and what the process was. He was upset that he did not know about it sooner.

I thought for sure he would be at the courtroom, comforting and supporting him. In the courtroom, her father and I are holding her hands as everything is said, and then she is given the opportunity to speak. She spoke about the abuse and what it did to her. The judge is moved and looks very puzzled. I get courage to speak as well and implore the judge to give more time as his sentencing. I am so proud of my daughter. The judge turns to ask the prosecutor why the sentencing is so lenient, given the horrible things he is hearing. The prosecutor says that he is new to the case and will get up to date in a few minutes. He then explains that there was a hung jury and that this was the best deal they could come up with. The judge shook his head and then continued with the sentencing.

He was handcuffed and taken out by the police, transported to the jailhouse. We went out to eat afterwards but barely had any appetite. We both told her how proud we are of her and that she spoke very well.

My oldest daughter has been singing and playing the piano since she was small. She is now our worship leader at church and has a few sisters that help her sing in the choir. It is a true blessing to see how strong she is. What the devil intended to destroy her with is the same thing she uses to praise God with. She has spoken out about her experience and other girls have come forward and talked to her about their dramatic experiences also. She says it feels good when you can help someone that you understand. Her desire is to study and become a psychologist and help other children that have gone through abuse or have a disability. I know that whatever she majors in and works in she will be of great help.

My son and youngest daughter are growing up so quickly. They are incredible. It amazes me to see how different my parenting is now. Not that I think I was a bad mother with my oldest daughter; I just worked too much. I worked three jobs and her grandmothers really raised her, not me.

When we lived with her dad, she was mostly with her grandma. Then when we lived with my parents, she was cared for by her grandparents, all day at their restaurant. The little time that I did have with her was treasured. Now with these two little ones, I have all the time in world to be with them. I feel some guilt from time to time because of it. I am just in a better position now, that is all.

Our son is impacted by the preaching he hears. He decides he wants to preach also. He is very smart is always wanting to learn more. I decide I will help him make that a reality. I spend lots of time with him, and jot things down as he tells me what is on his mind. He can go on and on forever, so I help him gather his thoughts and put them in order. I then find anecdotes that go with the theme or subject he is focusing on, and have him either watch or tell it to him over and over until he understands it. He learns it and is able to say it in his preaching. I love how confident he is. It is sad that we lose that confidence as we age.

My son preaches at our home church, and he was invited to go to another church and preach. He was very nervous, yet he did an excellent job. I am so proud of him. He is fascinated by everything he learns. Right now is learning two new languages.

My smallest daughter also is drawn to sing and play the piano. She is following in her sister's footsteps. She is very loveable and knows what she wants.

She was born with green eyes and very light hair. My husband says that his mother had red hair and that is where she must have inherited it. To this day her eyes turn gray in the summer, and she has reddish, very light colored hair. My cousins tease me that she is adopted because she does not look me at all. I love to say my children are EXTRAordinary, because they are. They are so special and are going to do great things for this world. I feel so privileged to have the opportunity of molding them and helping them become great people.

I instill the word of God in their lives, so they know that they have a purpose for living. Our greatest heritage that we leave them has to be the belief in God. I see them so young and with the way the world is, I cannot help but feel sad that they will not play and experience the same things that I did. They have all the knowledge of the world at their fingertips and that is frightening.

Chapter 13

Departure

It has been two years since I lost my husband. His departure was sudden and unexpected. My kids miss him so much. It is so difficult to explain to them what happened. Life has a way of completely shattering you when you least expect it. My husband was such a great person; I fell in love with him because of his big, remarkable heart. He loved to help out anyone that was in need. Always giving and always helpful is how we will remember him.

Although our last interaction was the most painful and awful memory I have of us together, I try not to think about it. I would like to think that all the good he did overweighed the one bad thing he did, but in this instance, it does not.

Addiction has a way of changing people. They do not care about consequences. Unfortunately, substance addiction damages not only the users but also whole families. I have seen it destroy great men that had so much potential and greatness. When I think of him, I think of only the great times we had and everything I learned from him. He was a noble man that came and brought so much love and happiness to our lives. He lives in my heart and thoughts always. I wish with all my heart that he would have been stronger in his thoughts and decisions. He made many mistakes in his life. Many mistakes were out of ignorance. Others, unfortunately, were made because he did not think about the consequences. I have found myself in a state of unforgiveness towards him. Although he is gone, I need to forgive him. One night I was in bed when a message came through from one of my cousins. My cousin has the tendency of calling and coming to visit at the precise moment we need her. I believe that she is so connected to her intuition and with her spirit that she listens to it. She sends me a message that comes with a video about our heart: "The Power of the Heart." She purchased it and sends it to me.

I watch it and instantly start to weep; I ask God to forgive me for not being a good enough wife to him, in my eyes. I wasn't enough to fill his void. I start to really analyze myself and ask if I listen to my heart. I see my role in his defeat. I knew in my heart that he was not well, and I didn't listen to it. In this video it talks about the power of our heart, and how it has the power to know what is coming. We need to listen to our heart. The Book of Daniel says,

"Then said he unto me, Fear not, Daniel: for from the first day that thou didst set thine heart to understand, and to chasten thyself before thy God, thy words were heard, and I am come for thy words" (Daniel 10:12).

I mediate and start to think that maybe if I had listened to it, I would have done certain things or taken different action. Sometimes I think we ignore what our heart is telling/asking us to do. I do not like to dwell on the things I cannot change. I make a conscious decision to be intentional about the things I say and do. Through all these experiences I have learned to become bold. To be bold in my actions, to be bold when I speak and when I want something. I was and am the kind of person that wants something and just goes for it. I do not look at the limitations; they do not exist. I am not afraid to speak up for injustice and to put myself out there. I have learned to trust and listen to my heart. I am aware that I have a lot more left to live and learn. Philippians 3:13 says,

"Brethren, I do not count myself to have apprehended; but one thing I do, forgetting those things which are

behind and reaching forward to those things which are ahead."

I know that I cannot change the past and there is nothing to gain by dwelling on what I could have done. I treasure only the good memories I had with him.

I was inspired to write this book mostly because I want my children to know the struggles. I want them to be aware and comprehend all that I was able to overcome. While writing this, at times I found myself in tears, because of the many things that I had blocked out of my memory. They were now suddenly intentionally brought to my mind and thoughts. It's been a great journey thus far.

As women, we have the ability to give birth and to nourish our children. We are incredibly strong and often do not even know it. Whenever something is presented to us we see the whole picture, yet sometimes we doubt ourselves. We are categorized as the weaker sex, however I believe we are the stronger ones in many ways. We manage to not die in labor, to raise our children, and work to contribute to our households. In some instances, we may contribute more to it economically. Even though we do so much, we need to become stronger in the sense of building and helping our husbands. We must be able to adapt to any situation. We must be able to defeat anything that attacks us. We must be able to endure it all.

"You therefore must endure hardship as a good soldier of Jesus Christ" (II Timothy 2:3).

As a mother I know that everything I do will affect my children and my grandchildren one day. I try to set a good example, but sometimes I fail. What I do know is that my children, family, and friends will see me keep getting up after each knockout. I'm thankful that I have a fighter in me, and with God's help she will prevail. We have been placed in the fire and still can smile. We have been torn apart over and over, and still we can trust. Our hearts have been ripped out, not just once, but many times, and we still can love.

It is said best in the words of Elizabeth Edwards:

"Resilience is accepting your new reality even if it's less good than the one you had before. You can fight it, you can do nothing but scream about what you have lost, or you can accept that and try to put together something that's good."

Reflections

Abuse is the improper use or the use for a bad purpose, misuse, cruel and violent treatment of a person. When we enter a relationship, it is because we want to make each other happy and are in love with one another. We sometimes mistake attention for love. We ignore or don't want to see the truth. We create our own reality that does not exist, and we live in our fantasy. It takes time to break free from this vicious cycle. I went back over and over because I thought there would be a change. However, there was no acceptance or recognition on his part, that anything was wrong. In order for there to be a change, there has to be admission of wrongdoing, the understanding that you need help. What I personally have learned is that you cannot assume a person that is being abused is going to leave their abuser. Our obligation and responsibility are to help when we see or know something is wrong and someone is being abused.

Child molestation is the sexual assault or abuse of a minor. The predator has usually been molested and continues the cycle until they are caught. This is one of the most destructive patterns that can happen, and the victim heals at their own pace. A victim of molestation is usually filled with guilt and shame. For some reason or another they believe that they provoked the abuse, which is never the truth! I have learned that there are not clear signs of molestation because the victim at times can hide it and will never want to talk about it because of embarrassment.

Abandonment is the most common issue in people. It creates a fear of rejection. No one enjoys being rejected. We all want to be accepted. We all fear it from time to time, in our relationships, jobs, projects, etc. It is all about building our self-esteem. God made us in His imagine. We are fearfully and wonderfully made!

Acknowledgements

I want to thank God for letting this dream of mine to become a reality. Special thanks to my editor, Liz Sarmiento, for taking the time to read the draft. She was able to keep my story and make the corrections and suggestions needed. Thank you to my wonderful family and my great friends that gave me so much support. I love you all dearly.

References

Holy Bible, English Standard Version
Holy Bible, New King James Version
Wikipedia
D.H. Sidebottom: "Stars can't shine without darkness"
Survival quote Danny Boyle
The Power of the Heart by Baptist de Pape

Made in the USA
Columbia, SC
20 July 2020